*Beckett at 60*

Sketch of Samuel Beckett by Avigdor Arikha 1965.

# Beckett at 60

## A FESTSCHRIFT

John Calder, ed

CALDER AND BOYARS

LONDON

*First published in Great Britain 1967*
*by Calder and Boyars Ltd.,*
*18, Brewer Street, London, W.1.*

© *Calder and Boyars, 1967*

MADE AND PRINTED IN GREAT BRITAIN
BY WILLMER BROTHERS LIMITED, BIRKENHEAD

# *Contents*

INTRODUCTION
*John Calder*                                                         1

## PART I   *Reminiscences*

THE THIRTIES
*A. J. Leventhal*                                                     7

A BLOOMLEIN FOR SAM
*Maria Jolas*                                                        14

FIRST MEETING WITH SAMUEL BECKETT
*Jerôme Lindon*                                                      17

MY COLLABORATION WITH SAMUEL BECKETT
*Marcel Mihalovici*                                                  20

WORKING WITH SAMUEL BECKETT
*Jack MacGowran*                                                     23

THE FIRST NIGHT OF WAITING FOR GODOT
*Harold Hobson*                                                      25

IN SEARCH OF BECKETT
*John Fletcher*                                                      29

WAITING FOR BECKETT
*Alan Schneider*                                                     34

## PART II   *Critical Examinations*

SAMUEL BECKETT'S POEMS
*Martin Esslin*                                                      55

PROGRESS REPORT 1962-65
*Hugh Kenner*                                                        61

v

# PART III *Tributes*

BECKETT THE MAGNIFICANT
*Madeleine Renaud* 81

MY DEAR SAM
*Robert Pinget* 84

BECKETT
*Harold Pinter* 86

PERSONAL NOTE
*Charles Monteith* 87

IN CONNECTION WITH SAMUEL BECKETT
*Fernando Arrabal* 88

*A Propos* SAMUEL BECKETT
*Philippe Staib* 89

TRIBUTE
*Aidan Higgins* 91

ALL THE LIVELONG WAY
*Mary Hutchinson* 93

SAMUEL BECKETT
*Alan Simpson* 96

A LETTER
*Jocelyn Herbert* 98

LAST TRIBUTE
*George Devine* 99

vi

# List of Illustrations

SKETCH OF SAMUEL BECKETT
BY ARIKHA                                    *Frontispiece*

SAMUEL BECKETT AT HIS
MOTHER'S KNEE                               *facing* p. 24

PHOTOGRAPH OF SAMUEL
BECKETT 1951                                *facing* p. 25

SAMUEL BECKETT AT REHEARSAL                 *facing* p. 40

THE VIEW FROM SAMUEL
BECKETT'S HOUSE                             *facing* p. 41

*Decorations to Half Titles
by Henri Hayden*

# Introduction

Samuel Beckett was sixty on the 13th of April nineteen sixty-six, a Wednesday as it happens, and not a Friday, for he was born on a Friday the thirteenth. And not only a Friday the thirteenth, but a *Good* Friday the thirteenth, which will seem proper enough to many of his readers, for if he seeks to flee the cross, it undoubtedly pursues him in his work, whether in the gospel ruminations of Vladimir, the blasphemies of Molloy or the total terror of the last paragraphs of *How It Is*. And this Beckettian fleeing to encounter, this paradoxical dualism, which hangs about the work and the reluctant figure of Mr. Beckett himself, must also serve as an excuse for this festschrift coming into being.

Books on Samuel Beckett's work are coming out like induced hailstorms to awaken the wasteland, good books, bad books, indifferent books, helpful books, unnecessary books, misleading books, books written very often when the writer could not care less whether it ever gets published or read. The compulsion to immerse oneself in the Beckett world, to study it, to come to know it better, understand it better, love it better, hate it better, to escape from all other worlds in it better, is caused by a fascination that Mr. Beckett would do much to be rid of. If the fascination gets into your system there is no cure, except the one cure, as Molloy would say. Mr. Beckett does not want the books; and the authors of them, whether intimate with their subject or not, know perfectly well that he does not want them, and yet they cannot refrain from bringing them into being; perhaps for the same reason that he him-

1

self cannot refrain from bringing new work into being, pushing out the tiny enormous boundaries of his world, that dust-bowl of hope and oasis of despair that makes the most compulsive reading of our time, once the language has been mastered and once we have learned the rhythms with which the Beckett world breathes. More books have been written on Christ, Napoleon and Wagner, in that order, than on any-one else. I predict that by 2000 A.D. Beckett may well rank fourth if the present flood of Beckett literature keeps up. And all this for an Irish writer who has reached a bare sixty, who one of the more eminent Sunday paper critics 'investigated' not so long ago in order to advise his readers whether to try it or not, and decided better not. He could not have found a better way to endear himself to S.B. and we of the present volume know only too well what icy fires we may set raging by putting together this 'tribute'. Some of the original contributors had second thoughts and wanted to withdraw their contributions, others insisted on cutting them, still others thought it wiser not to deliver. For to be honest we are all overawed, through respect, for the prophet from Dublin, and the closer we may be to the man and the greater our affection for him, the more we fear to hurt him through praise and offend him through emotion.

The fascination of the Beckett country lies largely in the dualism, and it is for that reason endlessly chewable. Mr. Beckett drops a hint now and again, and another door of end-less possibilities opens. As one who never felt any great need to trace the references in *The Waste Land*, I cannot resist flying back to the text to see what light a new glimmer will cast on a passage in Beckett Land. Not that we are dealing with obscurities. Beckett's plots are good, understandable, in-teresting plots, his situations are believable, his characters quickly become old friends. But we can also fill up the wilder-nesses with their histories, with the flora and fauna that the casual eye often misses in the present, the apparent inevit-ability of what may happen there in the future. The levels are bottomless. With Beckett, re-examination is somehow always worth-while doing, or rather there is no way of not doing it

once his work has caught hold of you. The dualism lies in the
paradox and the converse is also true. The more he shrinks his
world the more he enlarges it. The more he hides himself the
more he reveals himself, and our own situation takes on a new
aspect. The more he wallows in the muck the more he extends
our idea of beauty. The more he removes his centre of gravity
from the body physical, the solider the shuddering flesh becomes. The more he plunges us to the depths of despair the
brighter burns our need to hope. The more abstract the more
concrete, and the more apparently difficult, the more reward-
ingly simple the content . . . and the emotion. One could go
on for ever.

And therefore this book. It is not put together for the benefit of its subject who will chuck it away in disgust and who is
no more interested in being sixty than he was interested in
being one. It is not published for the benefit of the publisher
who will do as well out of it as the publisher of the narrator
of *From An Abandoned Work*. It is written for the
benefit of the contributors, who would honestly prefer the
author not to read what they have said, but who want to say
basically that they love him, or admire him, or that they are
grateful to him for making it possible to be grateful for something in our unspeakable century, by simply creating a little
body of print than no man can read from beginning to end
and still say, 'I am the same person. I am unchanged.' I can
think of no other living writer of whom I could say this, ad-
miring many.

And I suppose that it is incidently written for like-minded
readers, members of a strange club, each with his favourite
phrases of caustic humour or satisfying disgust; for future re-
searchers; for a public that may get hooked a little earlier by
its existence; for the curious; and for those with malice towards what Beckett represents on the current literary scene,
who may find some ammunition in it, at least I hope so, because they have done him much good in the past.

And now a word about the book itself. The illustrations by
Arikha and Henri Hayden are the tributes of distinguished
painters who are also old friends. Like M. Pinget, Mr. Pinter

3

and others, they have been circumspect in observing the decorum of the occasion. The first section of reminiscences gives a pretty good all-round picture of the man behind the work, what he is like to work with, the quality of the mind, the warmth of the person. The second makes valuable additional critical material available, essential to the Beckett addict: Martin Esslin tackles Beckett's poems in depth for the first time, one part of his work that has been consistently underrated; and Hugh Kenner, who has written (like John Fletcher) an indispensible book on Beckett, brings his past studies up to date. The shorter tributes are very varied, as are their authors. The last, short, very moving one from George Devine was dictated a few days before he died. They were fond of each other and the last sentence evokes their author as much as their subject; heartbreak is the word that best describes Samuel Beckett's quality in his writing, heartbreak in the Schubertian sense; generosity as Mr. Devine points out is the primary quality of the man.

John Calder

# PART I

## REMINISCENCES

# The Thirties

A. J. LEVENTHAL

For ordinary living we have to come to terms with memory; its unreliability is proved a thousand times in one's life. We have Proust's authority backed by Beckett that as an instrument of evocation voluntary memory is a very poor relation of involuntary remembrance. Writing on this subject in his work on Proust, Beckett says that the conscious effort to recall the past 'provides an image as far removed from the real as the myth of our imagination or the caricature furnished by direct perception'. These are severe words. It is not given to many and not often to those who are the lucky receptacles of involuntary messages from lost time to be able to use this gracious gift of the muse in their work as writers or for personal satisfaction. The Proustian miracle is, well, a miracle. His *madeleine* did more for literature than the saint of the same name, with the best will in and out of the world, could do for me. At best, all I could expect is that the smell of a *gauloise* in Dublin might open a Parisian wound or evoke a *nuit folle*. The sound of an Irish accent in Paris would do nothing more for me than remind me of say an exhibitionist poet or a Garda on point duty in College Green.

The other day walking along the Boulevard St. Michel I noticed the Café de l'Arrivée opposite the Luxembourg Gardens and suddenly recalled Sam telling me that it was there he had written his first prose book. I remembered too that at that time there was little money in the Beckettian purse and that heating was expensive. This explained the café as workshop. Trivial as a memory job, I was glad I didn't drop the item

7

into the gutter-water. Back in my apartment I reached for the nearest copy of *Proust* and found that its date of first publication 1931 was well within the chosen decade. I admired the John Calder title page with its chaste caps. and broad nude spaces. I was delighted to find that the book was printed in Ireland. This must have unconsciously suggested the adjective I used to describe the Roman capitals. I was seemingly unaccountably unhappy about the great expanse of white and found the original Chatto & Windus edition. I found the reason for my unease. The plunging dolphin on the title page of the earlier publication was symbolic of the name given to the series and the ornamental tree in the reprint could easily pass as a Beckett symbol. *Mais ce n'est pas là la question.* What was lacking was the quotation from Leopardi : *E fango è il mondo.* This should not have been omitted if only out of piety to the memory of Joyce who loved it because of the possible *double entendre.* I am rich in Beckett editions and found that the German version also had also banned Leopardi. I still wonder why.

I am now in Dublin planted in one of the Four Courts on the quays whisked there by the occult forces of free association. It is the year 1937 or thereabouts. I have been supoenaed as a witness in a libel action : Sinclair v. Gogarty. All Dublin was there and I would have never been admitted if I had not been summoned. The plaintiff claimed damages from Gogarty for statements in *Walking down Sackville street* that were hurtful to his reputation. The defendant was of course the archetype of Bollocky Mulligan in Joyce's *Ulysses.* I see Samuel Beckett in the witness box. He had had an easy time with Sinclair's counsel the previous day but with one Fitzgerald on the other side he is not doing well. Sam's honesty with this legal fox is being used to blacken his character and invalidate his earlier testimony. Yes, he lives in Paris. He has no strong views on the existence of God. He has written a book on a Frenchman called Prowst by counsel but corrected by Sam. The lawyer, turning towards the jury : 'This man Prowst or (with a knowing look at Dublin's judging citizens) Proust is he not the author of an immoral book?' I can't remember Sam's reply. It didn't matter by this time. It is soon established that the witness himself is author of a banned book (the title was enough; no censor would risk his immortal soul by reading it) called *More Pricks than Kicks*. Counsel dare not speak its name. The Dublin evening papers carried banner headlines: THE ATHEIST FROM PARIS.

A little later there occurred that extraordinary incident when, returned to Paris and walking on the boulevard in Montparnasse, Sam was stabbed by some *mec* from the *milieu*—a sort of Gidean *acte gratuit*. As the poet laureate brightly said: 'Along the electric wires the message came.' Headlines in the Dublin daily papers! The Bailey Restaurant supplied the oysters for Gogarty and his guests to celebrate the event.

All this must be voluntary memory and is, be assured, neither myth nor, I hope, caricature. It may well lack interest or be long known by writers on Samuel Beckett and considered too trivial for use. I write this note more or less within the social framework demanded of me by the editor and am unaware as to how other contributors are paying homage to one of the greatest literary figures of our day. And so I persist in trusting my memory for I have kept no diary and am perforce thrown back to rummaging in the dustbin of my mind in the hope of finding something valuable. Ragpickers according to Giraudoux always found something in the good old days.

The fun Sam must have had writing his prize poem *Whoroscope*! The title might possibly have been different if there were no Joyce living in the quarter. But the work itself? I can hear him chuckling at the opening lines: 'What's that/An egg?/By the brothers Boot it stinks fresh,/Give it to Gillot.' 'Cold mutton,' said Oscar Wilde when he was seen leaving a brothel, 'tell them that in England.' Tell them that in Ireland, almost says the note about the Boot brothers whom he credits with the refutation of Aristotle in Dublin in 1640. As for Gillot, the note neatly echoes Villiers de l'Isle Adam. He is the valet who does our sums for us. Some critics have not been quite fair. Ruby Cohn sits too heavily on the comic pan of her scales whilst Hugh Kenner dismisses too cavalierly the work of the thirties as pedantic and precious. There is real fun in his

9

poem on Time and it does not help the argument to say that B. has a higher average of footnotes in *Whoroscope* than Eliot in his *The Waste Land*. The notes are part of the amusement, just as they are in *Watt*.

But I step out of my terms of reference when I enter the literary lists. *Whoroscope* may be the result of years of reading (the Whistler defence) but it was physically the work of one night—a whole night. The young *lecteur* was in the rue d'Ulm ministering to the cultural needs of the students whose school claims paradoxically to be normal as well as superior. His friend Tom McGreevy suggested the possibility of making £10 if he competed for the prize offered by Nancy Cunard but this was the last day for submission, a day in 1929. I can easily imagine the two friends staggering happily at dawn to the rue Guénégaud where Nancy lived to deposit the MSS in her box so that the rules of the competition might be observed. The latter, by the way, was caught in the verbal vortex of the decade in her search for a poem on Time to be published by the Hours Press. Richard Aldington was one of the judges. It is worth recording. Let it be added to the credit side of a wrongly neglected writer.

His Ecole Normale spell ended, Sam is back again in Dublin. He is introducing French literature to the young Irishry at Trinity College. His silences in company were as marked as James Joyce's but curiously this was no impediment to his success as a lecturer. Later one of his students, Leslie Daiken (poet, expert on children's toys and games, died 1965) who showed me the notes he had taken at lectures, told me how Sam would stand for minutes staring through the window and then throw a perfectly constructed sentence to his crumb picking avid audience. To judge from the notes there was no obscurity. He passed on his own love for Racine just as his own professor Rudmose-Brown had done for him but with a greater clarity. The characters in *Andromaque* are shown chasing each other round the circumference of a circle. If it were a philosophy class there would have been a diagram likewise to help understanding. I am thinking of his earlier demonstration of Vico's place in *Finnegans Wake*. But as B.

said in the same *Exagmination* essay : 'The danger is in the neatness of identification.' There are circles and cycles. That the diagram has significance for our author is clear from their presence in the text of one of the mimes (Act without Words 2) whilst in *Imagination morte, imaginez* the reader can construct the material situation from the precise geometrical data.

In parenthesis and a new paragraph may I ask when are we going to have an illustrator of B.'s work? Both Blake and Dali have interpreted Dante; it would require a mixture of both of their qualities, a power of illumination plus magic. I am not forgetting the admirable abstractions with which Arikha has decorated *Textes pour Rien* but the abstract is finally more ornamental than interpretive.

Academism was not to B.'s liking and after a few terms he fled. The College wits murmured that he wrote his resignation on a scroll of bumph but those in authority wailed because with him went the College master key. All they could do was to change all the locks and appoint me in his place. They were to call him back briefly in 1959 to pay him the greatest honour in their gift, an honorary doctorate. If they had read *Watt* they would have laughed with him at the permutation and combination extravanza which made bold to assess what happened when the members of the Board exchanged looks on hearing what the unfortunate research student Louit had to say.

B.'s hegira took him round various European countries with stays in London from which city an urgent postcard. Would I betake me to the Dublin Post Office and measure the height from the ground of Cuchulain's arse? This ancient Irish hero, imagined by Yeats as standing beside those who fought in the G.P.O. in 1916, has a statue erected to him there 'to mark the place/By Oliver Sheppard done'. A crowd gathered round as I knelt with a tape measure to carry out my task and was lucky to get away without arrest. Later I read in *Murphy*:

'Neary ... was recognized in the General Post Office contemplating from behind the statue of Cuchulain.

11

Neary had bared his head as though the holy ground meant something to him. Suddenly he flung aside his hat, sprang forward, seized the dying hero by the thighs and began to dash his head against his buttocks, such as they are.'

It was essential for our author, who is nothing if not meticulous, to know whether this violent gesture was in fact possible.

Much of Sam's time in the thirties was taken up by translation to keep warm and stay himself with naggins. Some of this work was lost. Rimbaud's *Bateau Ivre* paid for by E. W. Titus disappeared with the editor of *This Quarter*. B. is inclined to despise these renderings 'Cette vieille foutaise alimentaire' is how he inscribes my copy of *An Anthology of Mexican Poetry*. These translations from the Spanish commissioned by Unesco in the forties were only published in 1958. Written when the budget was knapp, their appearance ten years later when fame had come in another literary field must have been an irritant. But the self denigration is unjustified. He is just as effective here as in his translations of his own work where he sacrificed the literal to the living.

It was in the thirties (where this paper should be fixed) when the economic shoe pinched just as badly that he made a name for himself in a small but exclusive circle as an interpreter of French surrealist poetry. Many have tried but few have succeeded as he has in capturing Eluard's magic simplicity :

> She is standing on my lids
> And her hair is in my hair
> She has the colour of my eye
> She has the body of my hand
> In my shade she is engulfed
> As a stone against the sky

This is the first of two stanzas of the poem 'Lady Love'. It is published with many others in the surrealist number of *This Quarter* (1932) in the editorial of which we read : 'We cannot refrain from singling out Mr. Samuel Beckett's work for special acknowledgement. His rendering of the Eluard and Breton poems in particular is characterizable only in superlatives.'

Earlier he was one of a band of illustrious writers who teamed up to translate a fragment of *Anna Livia Plurabelle* into French. Unaccountably this work—a remarkable performance—has had no more permanent form since its original printing in the May number 1931 of the *Nouvelle Revue Française*.

There are many who will not listen to any disparagement of the early work. They pooh pooh the pundits who cry pedantry and esoteric wit. They revel, when they can find them, in those prose pieces in *Transition* not reprinted and clamour for a new edition of *More Pricks than Kicks*. What bibliophiles call ephemerae are only such because no one has bothered to gather the fugitive pieces and bind them in boards. The author says no? It would be a good title.

# A Bloomlein for Sam

MARIA JOLAS

The young man was fondling with pride his new book, a paper-back edition of *Finnegans Wake,* which I had not yet seen. I asked to look at it.

On the fly-leaf, copied by the owner, I read : 'Joyce is not writing about something : he is writing something. When the sense is sleep, the words go to sleep. When the sense is dancing, the words dance.' Signed : Samuel Beckett. 'Are you sure,' I asked somewhat incredulously, 'that Beckett wrote that?' The young man was almost sure, but he had not noted the reference. But I myself felt sure : it could only have been when he was quite young.

Having already begun to brush up on a rather distant past in order to contribute my modest bloomlein to Sam's birthday bouquet, I happened to have with me at that very moment the June 1929 issue of *Transition* in which I had started to read again, after many years, *Dante ... Bruno, Vico ... Joyce,* the first article by Sam that we had published. An hour later, in my favourite rue de Rennes *tabac,* and in spite of the heavily amorous scene that was being enacted at the next table, I had come upon the quoted passage in its brilliant context. I was rather pleased with my find. I had felt almost certain that Sam had written no literary criticism since before the war, but I might well have been mistaken. Actually, the last would appear to have been an article on Dennis Devlin, which appeared in *Transition* no. 27 in 1938.

Returning to this distant source explained for me too why I myself seemed to have so little clear recollection of Sam at

14

the time of his first appearance in *Transition*. In 1929 we were still living in Colombey-les-Deux-Eglises—a more charming place then, I imagine, than the miniature police state it has become since—and although I was a very active secretary and translator for *Transition,* I also had a young child and was expecting another, so that my place was decidedly 'in the home' and I had little first-hand contact with the editorial world of Paris contributors. I do remember well, however, with what excitement Joyce's recommendation of the highly gifted young Irishman's manuscript was received by my husband, and how fond he became of its author as he came to know him better.

In 1931 we moved back to Paris and gradually I began to swim up to the surface of unrelieved domestic and secretarial duties. I remember that we even gave a fairly large 'party' at which Sam was so to speak present, only so silent, so with-drawn, that my robust Kentucky conviviality was discon-certed, and I could think of little to say or do other than to ply him with refreshments.

There were other occasional meetings during those years : chez Joyce of course and, if I remember rightly, chez Peggy Guggenheim and John Holmes. But Sam usually remained a silent partner.

In 1932 I founded the *Ecole Bilingue de Neuilly* which was to become as it were the *deus ex machina* behind my move, in September 1939, to the Allier where, because their grandson was a pupil in the school, Nora and James Joyce joined me for Christmas. When Easter found them still there Sam was invited to join us, and he did so.

The school was temporarily housed in a spacious and prob-ably once well-appointed early 19th century country house, and with the sixty or so children and teachers all away on vacation there was more than room for our little group. By now, for Joyce, Sam had become a close friend and his pres-ence at that moment of personal distress and general anxiety was particularly welcome. My memory of that fortnight is one of soft spring days marked by a sort of gentle laziness broken by occasional music, home-made as well as recorded. Our inevitable awareness that the 'phoney' phase of the war was coming to a close was relegated momentarily to the background.

These then were the stepping-stones to my now thirty-five-year-old friendship with Sam Beckett. Today, even, I can't say really that time has brought much greater actual contact between us, except for the immediate post-war period, when we worked together on some translations. But there remains from those earlier years a closely woven web of shared affections and loyalties which is intact, and which I value because I know that it will not alter.

And when I read Sam today, however different from Joyce's —and it is absolutely different—his writing nevertheless seems to bridge the gap for me between now and Joyce. I hear the same soft Dublin voice, I sense the same vast cultural past, the same ferocious but as often very gentle irony, the same humanity and rare wit that makes me laugh out loud as I read. Like Joyce he is also a Christ-haunted man, not yet of the new barbarism.

But there is a fundamental difference. Joyce could still say yes, whereas Sam's answer is definitely no.

# First Meeting with Samuel Beckett

JERÔME LINDON

One day in 1950, a friend of mine, Robert Carlier, told me: 'You should read the manuscript of an Irish writer who writes in French. He is called Samuel Beckett. Six publishers have already refused him.' I had been running my publishing company, *Les Editions de Minuit,* for two years. A few weeks later I noticed three manuscripts on my desk: they were *Molloy, Malone Meurt* and *L'Innommable,* and bore the name of an unknown author that already looked familiar.

It was from this day that I knew that I was going to be a publisher, that is to say a *real* publisher. From the first line, 'I am in my mother's room. It's I who live there now. I don't know how I got there'—from the first line, the overwhelming beauty of the text assaulted me. I read *Molloy* in a few hours as I had never read a book before. It was not a novel that had been published by one of my colleagues, a sacred masterpiece that I, as a publisher, could never have anything to do with: it was an unpublished manuscript, and not only unpublished, but one that had been refused by several publishers. I could not believe it.

I met Suzanne, his wife, the next day, and I told her that I would like to bring out the three books as quickly as possible, but that I was not very well off. She agreed to take the contracts back to Samuel Beckett and to return them to me signed. It was the 15th November 1950.

Samuel Beckett came to see us in the office a few weeks later. Suzanne tells me that he returned home looking very unhappy. When she showed her surprise, believing that he was

17

upset by the terms of this first contract with his publisher, he replied that to the contrary he had found us all very sympathetic, and that he was only in despair at the realization that the publication of *Molloy* would lead to our bankruptcy.

The book came out on 15th March. The printer, a Catholic from Alsace, worried that the book would be prosecuted for offending good morality, had prudently omitted to put his name at the end of the volume.

A few days later I wrote to Sam to ask for a photograph of himself, and also for a short story which he had mentioned, with the idea of offering both to a newspaper.

He replied with the following letter :

10.IV.51

Dear M. Lindon,

Your letter of yesterday to hand. Most cordial thanks for your generous advance.[1]

I had the photograph taken this afternoon. It will be ready after tomorrow and I will send it to you just as soon.[2]

I know that Roger Blin wants to put on the play.[3] He has requested a subsidy for it. I very much doubt that he will get it. Let us wait for *Godot,* but not for tomorrow.

The story, of which the first part under the title *La Fuite* has appeared in *Les Temps Modernes,* is at your disposal.[4] Can it wait until my return? It is my first work in French (in prose). *Le Calmant* that Madame

---

[1] The 'generous advance' in question came to, if I remember rightly, 25,000 old francs (around £16).

[2] This photograph, the only one that was known to exist for many years up to this time, is reproduced facing page 25.

[3] This concerned the première of *Waiting for Godot* in Paris. Theatres had refused this play for a long time because there was 'neither a woman, nor a communist, nor a priest' in it. The first performance finally took place in January 1953.

[4] *Les Temps Modernes* had not continued publishing after the first part. This story appeared under the title *La Fin* in *Nouvelles Et Textes Pour Rien.* (Mr. Beckett has just completed the translation for English publication.)

Dumesnil has given to Monsieur Lambrichs, would perhaps be more suitable.[5] I leave the choice to you.

I am very pleased to hear that you want to bring out *L'Innommable* as rapidly as possible. As I told you, I prefer this last work, in spite of it having involved me in a mess of dirty sheets.[6] I am trying to get out of them. But I'm not succeeding. I do not know if it will be able to make a book. It will perhaps be a time for nothing.[7]

Allow me to say how much I am touched by the interest that you have shown in my work and by the difficulties that you are taking on yourself. And believe in my sincere and friendly regards.

Samuel Beckett

As Samuel Beckett may very well cast his eyes on this meagre little tribute, I do not dare to express the enormous admiration and affection that I have for him. He would be embarrassed and on that account I should be so too. But I would like this to be known, and only this : that in all my life I have never met a man in whom co-exist together in such high degree, nobility and modesty, lucidity and goodness. I would never have believed that anyone could exist who is at the same time so real, so truly great, and so good.

[5] George Lambrichs was at this time secretary to the Reading Committee of Les Editions de Minuit. *Le Calmant* has also appeared in *Nouvelles et Textes pour Rien*.

[6] Quoi qu'il m'ait mis dans de sales draps.

[7] In fact, these attempts eventually appeared under the title *Textes Pour Rien* (only now in 1967 translated into English.)

# My Collaboration with Samuel Beckett

MARCEL MIHALOVICI

---

I have worked together with Samuel Beckett on two occasions :
when I wrote the opera *Krapp* from his play *La Dernière
Bande* (*Krapp's Last Tape*) and when I wrote the music for
his 'radiophonic invention' *Cascando*. *Krapp* was composed
between 1959 and 1960, *Cascando* in 1963. I only wish to
recall at this time the memories of my work during the first of
these occasions and the part that the great writer played in it.
Eight or nine years ago, I asked Samuel Beckett one day to
write an opera libretto for me. He said that he felt himself in-
capable of doing such a work, but instead proposed to
me three texts which were at that time unpublished : these
were *Ceux Qui Tombent*, *La Dernière Bande* and a third
which had not yet been finished. My choice stopped at *La
Dernière Bande*. This was because I immediately realized the
new musical possibilities that were offered to me by such very
individual and varied techniques as were present in the
dramatic action of this unpublished play. I said so to Beckett.
I also realized the difficulties of execution. And in addition
I asked him if he would come to see me and bring with him
Roger Blin, one of his principal interpreters and directors, so
that he could act out the play in front of us several times over.
In this way, I was able to absorb the cadence of the text, its
rhythm and its length. And then I threw myself with lowered
head into my audacious plan of composition. Beckett's help
was, I can say, essential at that point. Because Beckett is a re-

markable musician—did you know it?—he possesses an astonishing musical intuition, an intuition that I often used in my composition. During the course of the long months when I was writing the score for *Krapp,* his many counsels were of enormous benefit to me. I was often reminded of what Darius Milhaud and Arthur Honegger had said of their collaboration with Paul Claudel, that in their case too the poet's musical intuition had enabled them to penetrate more easily into the secrets of the work that he had given them. Beckett on occasion caused me to make changes in what I showed him in the score, he either approved or disapproved, made me modify certain stresses in the vocal line, while at the same time helping me to look for others. It would be useless to say that I was able to understand all his suggestions and all his criticisms. But then, one fine day, after fourteen months of work, my score was finished. I shall always remember the astonishment of Beckett to whom I immediately showed it and who looked at the ten pages of his text spread out over an orchestral score of nearly 260 pages of music! And in spite of that, our opera, which in order to differentiate it from the stage play we called *Krapp* (or *The Last Tape*), barely lasts fifteen minutes longer than the play in its original form. It was then that I could see how useful the reading by Roger Blin and the advice of Samuel Beckett had been to me.

*Krapp* presented to a musician such as myself unaccustomed problems and a number of very different ones. The melancholy poetry which it releases, as well as its violent eruptions, offered me wonderful opportunities for musical contrast. And in addition, the very construction of Beckett's work, with its various moods, lyrical, aggressive, cynical, or merely contemplative, more than once indicated to me the structural sounds that I should adopt. There was above all the problem of the recorded tape (the voice of Krapp), accompanied by a real orchestra in the pit of the theatre, which made me face solutions, difficult but passionately interesting ones, which I am unable to expand on here. There was also the problem of the voice of Krapp as a young man (on tape) and of the old Krapp who is singing on the stage. I thought of giving the

21

latter long passages of *Sprechgesang,* which would allow the singer to adopt, here and there, the intonations of an old man, while the tape, other than during certain short interjections, or of certain phrases which could not be sung, would unwind to a real lyricism, a lyricism which would try to come near to the original, admirable Beckett text. The baritone William Dooley succeeded wonderfully well in giving to the role of Krapp these moments of release, with all their nuances, when he sang the role at the Bielefeld Opera, at the Theatre of the Nations in Paris, and at the Opera in Berlin.

I should like to say a word more about the German and English versions that Elmar Tophoven, the German translator of Beckett's work, and that Beckett himself made to the French prose that I used in composing *Krapp.* Beckett, being multilingual, was able here as well to supervise the long series of events very thoroughly. I was endlessly present at all these sessions, long ones, very long ones indeed, to give my advice regarding the vocal inflexions which had to be modified because of the translation. In fact, these new inflexions very often forced me to find vocal lines and stresses very different from those in my original score. And I also think that thanks to this knowledge, and to the profound intuition which my friend had of German and English, the translations did not cause any of the poetry of Krapp to be lost, that poetry which had originally seduced me in its French version, and that what we created are translations of a rare perfection in dramatic music.

# Working with Samuel Beckett

JACK MACGOWRAN

One of the common cries of old theatreland so often heard is 'Keep the author out!' I've bawled it myself more than once, and for very good reasons. There were also the very rare occasions when I shouted 'Bring the author in!' and again for very good reasons.

Samuel Beckett was in the forefront of this few, and I have never regretted this soul-cry. The need of actors, particularly in our time to know why they are saying what they are saying and doing what they are doing is a need that demands satisfaction so that as complete a form of communication as possible can be established between them and their audience, a need equally emphatic from the audience's point of view.

There is more than one way of performing certain plays, particularly those that break new ground and create new styles, but there is only one true way. The value of relationships in theatre today has a more definite importance than so-called 'plot' and dialogue, and relationship, frequently treated as secondary, is the primary key to the eventual performance.

Close collaboration with Samuel Beckett has made the performance of his works an experience which is both rewarding and illuminating. His own relationship with actors and directors, scenic designers and lighting men is first solidly established clearly by Mr. Beckett himself, so that when it comes to rehearsing text and movement, there is a marked understanding. Such collaboration brought the recent performance of 'Endgame' to Paris and the Royal Shakespeare, London, with the success one had always hoped for, and the more

23

Mr. Beckett himself discovered of the secrets of the theatre, the more he brought his own originality and ideas to it, adding definition and dimension to performances that might have otherwise been limited. His feeling for precision in inflection, rhythm and movement seems almost severe, but not for a moment does he restrict the imagination or inventive feeling of others, except where it is outside the framework of what is being interpreted. He creates a freedom in working which actors do not often enjoy in the theatre today, and this freedom is always the bedfellow of true discipline. His visual sense is so harmonious, that he cannot happily accept second best in acting, design, lighting or direction. In these matters he is extremely specific, as the balance of all the elements that result in the final product is a delicate but positive one.

Working with Sam Beckett is an exciting exploration. The impact of his radio plays, my first acquaintance with his work, aroused something long asleep in the recesses of my being, an impact which became more and more concentrated over the ensuing years as his novels, poems, essays, and plays focussed my interest with an intensity I had hardly thought myself capable of. All this seems what can be called inspiration, for indeed his work inspired me. This was rewarding enough, but meeting, knowing and working with Sam Beckett was and is a privilege for which I shall be forever grateful.

Talking to a young teenager recently about Sam Beckett's work, she summed up why his increasing popularity among younger audiences is so marked, when she said 'The more I read Sam Beckett and feel his compassion for the human condition, I realize that the magnitude of my own youthful and harrowing problems need no longer be a tortured secret, but can really be understood and shared, and my existence made much more tolerable.'

She spoke for countless numbers.

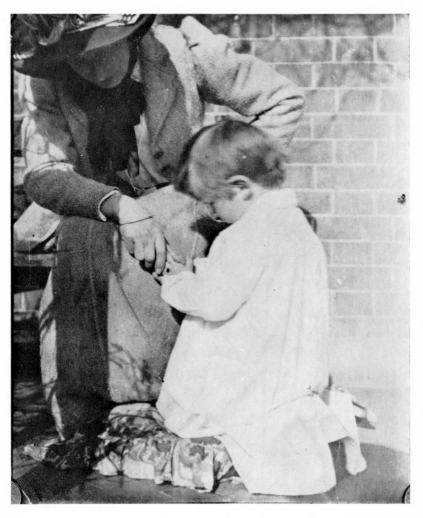

Samuel Beckett at his mother's knee. The earliest known
photograph. *Photograph by Dorothy Kay.*

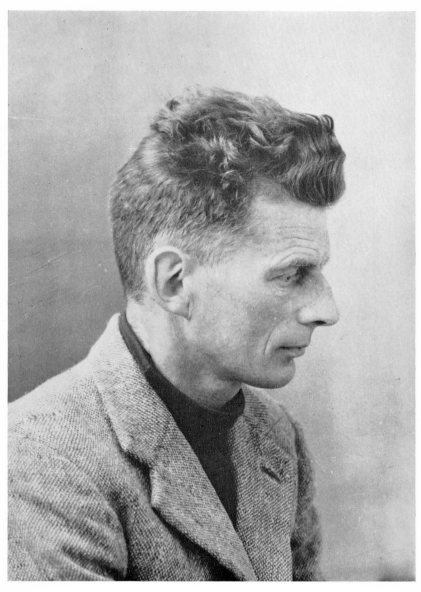

This photograph of Mr. Beckett, taken in 1951 is the one
referred to by Jerome Lindon on p. 18.

# The First Night of "Waiting for Godot"

HAROLD HOBSON

In my lifetime there have been three first performances of plays that have deeply influenced for good the course of the English drama. The earliest, and I think the most important of these, was the opening performance at the Arts Theatre on August 3rd, 1955 of Samuel Beckett's *Waiting for Godot*. *Waiting for Godot* was directed by Peter Hall, and presented by Donald Albery. This play knocked the shackles of plot from off the English drama. It destroyed the notion that the dramatist is God, knowing everything about his characters, and master of a complete philosophy answerable to all our problems. It showed that Archer's dictum that a good play imitates the audible and visible surfaces of life is not necessarily true. It revealed that the drama approximates, or can approximate, to the condition of music, touching chords deeper than can be reached by reason, and saying things beyond the grasp of logic. It renewed the English theatre in a single night.

I watched the performances of Paul Daneman, Peter Woodthorpe, Peter Bull, and Timothy Bateson at first with incomprehension, then with a troubled interest, and then with anxiety. The almost bare stage, empty except for a desolate tree, the two tramps worried by their boots, their bladders, their solitude, their constantly disappointed expectation of the arrival of the unexplained and probably inexplicable Godot seemed to hold no promise of a good story about interesting people, which was the sort of thing I had come to expect the

25

theatre, when on form, to tell me. No plot developed, no intrigue suggested itself, yet one of the character's preoccupation with why only one of the thieves at the Crucifixion was saved entered into and stirred my mind. It had associations and echoes of nobility. Gradually the feeling came over me that here was an author of no common quality. This feeling however did not seem to be shared by the audience at the Arts Theatre. Certain early lines in the play, such as 'I have had better entertainment elsewhere', provoked ironical laughter; and when one of the characters yawned, the yawn was repeated and amplified by a humorist in the stalls. Here and there one could identify sharp centres of disaffection, and now and again a playgoer would get up and stamp out of the theatre in anger and boredom.

All this made me unhappy. Lucky's extraordinary speech, in which all the wisdom and the knowledge of the world are jumbled to the pitiful end of incoherence and madness, was wonderfully delivered by Timothy Bateson, but it did not turn the tide of the audience's growing hostility. In the theatre that night was Margaret Ramsay, who has done as much as anyone to find and to encourage new young dramatists in England. I spoke to her a few days ago about the performance. She had read the play before, and had been profoundly moved by it. She had sent it to the Arts Council whose reader had returned it with contumely, describing it as rubbish. She says that she looked across at me during the first act, and saw me crumpled up in my seat, gloomy and miserable. She thought to herself, 'Oh God, he doesn't like it.' All I remember of this is that she came across to me in the interval and said, 'Allow the author to speak, Harold. All the critics are going to hate it.' To which I replied, unmemorably, 'I don't see why they should.' Anyway, Margaret Ramsay was right. The next morning the play got dreadful notices. On the following Sunday Kenneth Tynan and I spoke up for it. Some weeks later the Arts Council took the unusual step of writing a letter of apology for their blindness to its splendour.

After that first night I could not get *Waiting for Godot* out of my mind. I went to see it again and again, both at the Arts and at the Criterion, whither Donald Albery boldly transferred it. It ran for six months, though nearly every performance was interrupted by malcontents. I wrote of it several times, and was much criticized as a bore for doing so. The play itself continued to be violently attacked, and even my great friend Collie Knox joined the chorus of dispraise sung by men of less culture and intelligence.

But that first night at the Arts hung in my memory, and weeks afterwards I was still writing about Mr. Beckett and *Waiting for Godot* in *The Sunday Times*. On Saturday 25th I said : 'Mr. Samuel Beckett used to write in English, and then to translate into French. His first considerable work, *Murphy,* was a London novel of the seedy, sexy streets round King's Cross, the melancholy sheep in Hyde Park, and the four caged owls in Battersea. But the general English public would have none of Mr. Beckett, with the result that his chief production, *Molloy,* exists at the moment only in a foreign language.

'It was no wonder that he first wrote *Waiting for Godot* in a foreign language; and there are many people in this country dementedly determined that, if they have any influence at all, it is in a foreign language that he shall continue to write. At the Criterion is one of the most noble and moving plays of our generation, a threnody of hope deceived and deferred but never extinguished; a play suffused with tenderness for the whole human perplexity; with phrases that come like a sharp stab of beauty and pain; with strophes and anti-strophes as exquisite as any imagined by Cranmer; a play in which words "are not the polite contortions of twentieth century printers' ink. They are alive. They elbow their way onto the page, and glow and blaze and fade and disappear".

'What would you expect to be the reception accorded to this writer of English newly returned to the English stage? Would you not expect us to see him while he was yet a great way off, to run towards him, and to beg him to stay with us? Some people who really have the welfare of the English theatre at heart have in fact done precisely that; and their action has aroused such a frothing of bat-blind abuse as makes one despair of our ever being worthy of having a great dramatist again.

'I grieve that Mr. Collie Knox, a man whose wit and true gentleness of spirit I know and admire, has made himself the spokesman of this stupid and intolerant view. Phrases like "They are born astride of a grave"—phrases beyond the compass of any English prose dramatist at present writing in England—are to Mr. Knox incoherent, "a conglomeration of tripe", a "glorification of the gutless". It is this complacent inability to recognize the highest when we see it, this apparently natural enmity towards exaltation of the spirit, which for a moment checks one's heart. It is this attitude that is the reason why Olivier and Gielgud are playing Shakespeare, why Redgrave is playing Giraudoux, and Wolfit Hochwaelder. It is the reason why some of us are Francomaniacs. It has left *them* nothing else to do. It has left *us* little else to be.'

That was a true statement of the state of the English drama as it was when *Waiting for Godot* was produced, and as it would have remained had not the English Stage Company presented John Osborne's *Look Back in Anger* a few months later.

It was the second act of the play that clinched the matter. This second act, which did not mollify the audience, parallels and expands the themes of the first, so that finally when the young boy appears for the second time we realize that we have seen a work of perfect form and shape, classical in its accomplishment. It was the ending of the play, the boy's strange and exquisite courtesy, and Vladimir's awed raising of his hat and his exclamation, 'Christ have mercy upon us', on learning that the colour of Godot's beard was white, that finally sealed my admiration and affection. Mr. Daneman wrote to me some years later that the feeling I experienced from his performance was the exact opposite of that which he had wanted to induce. But from this I draw no conclusions.

# In Search of Beckett

JOHN FLETCHER

I first came across the name of Samuel Beckett eleven or so years ago, when a schoolfriend showed me a copy of *Waiting for Godot,* which had been provoking considerable discussion in the press. I read the play, and it intrigued me as much as it did other people at the time. I did not understand it, but it made an impact. A little later, during my first year at Cambridge, I went to see *Fin de partie* done in French at the Royal Court. It was during the vacation; one Sunday, I had read in *The Observer* that Beckett's new play was to have its world première that week, so on the day I went to the local station, bought a day excursion ticket to London, and went to the theatre box-office. I had not taken the precaution to book, and so, of course, all the seats were taken. This possibility had simply not occurred to me. I was stunned. 'But,' I protested, 'I've come all the way from Somerset to see this play, I just can't go back without seeing it.' They must have taken pity on me, for a seat was found, and I witnessed the first-night performance. On the milk-train that took me home that night, I meditated on my disappointment. As soon as I had read that the play was coming, I had felt I *had* to see it; to this day, I don't know what it was that drove me. But my seat had not been a very good one (naturally enough), and what with that, and the emotion, and the fact that my French was not then quite as good as it should have been to understand Beckett's very varied and poetic language, I had not derived as much pleasure from the performance as I had hoped. But I did not

29

forget Roger Blin's Hamm or Jean Martin's Clov, both of which were remarkable.

Soon afterwards, I saw a copy of *Molloy* in a Cambridge bookshop, the first Olympia Press edition, and I bought it. For one reason or another, I took a long time to get around to reading it. I had graduated and was doing postgraduate research at Toulouse University when I got down to it properly. I had been reading Jung just before that, and that helped me to understand something of what the novel was about, although it is now clear to me that I tended then to impose too neat a Jungian interpretation on it. Nevertheless, the book opened my eyes and I realized that here was a writer of genius.

He was still relatively little known, and so I decided to take 'Beckett's symbolism' as my research topic. Professor Dupont, who had heard *Godot* on the radio and been impressed, agreed to direct my studies. Eventually I took a Toulouse doctorate on Beckett's work, and my original idea about the symbolism gradually took the form of a book on the evolution of his fiction. My work soon put me in touch with other scholars, and when Raymond Federman suggested we collaborate on a full bibliography, I accepted at once. It was decided that he would concentrate on the criticism devoted to Beckett, while I would draw up the list of his complete works.

This was no easy matter. The existing lists made no claim to completeness, and Mr. Beckett himself had forgotten most of his early pieces. For I had been lucky, during a year spent in Paris, to meet him. It happened this way. I called on Professor Mayoux at the Sorbonne with a query I had, arising out of an essay he had written on Beckett. He advised me to see Geneviève Serreau, wife of the director and actor. She had a collection of press cuttings relating to the première of *Godot* at the Babylone Theatre which her husband had run. I called on her at the offices of the review *Les Lettres Nouvelles* and she very kindly let me see the dossier and take notes. She asked me if I'd met Beckett, and offered to introduce me. Not long after, I received a letter from him in which he said that he would be glad to give me whatever help he could with biographical and bibliographical material, but that he could not discuss his work and never did. This I knew already, and as the help I wanted was in fact the help he offered to give, I called to see him in his Paris flat the day mutually agreed upon.

I was very nervous, but he was, despite the rather abrupt tone of his letter, kindness itself. He obviously has to fend off unwelcome pestering, but once he has agreed to see you, he will go to great lengths to help. He answered fully all the questions I had noted to put to him, and gave me several clues that I followed up usefully in the following months. Then he suddenly produced the typescript, written in 1932, of his first novel, the unpublished *Dream of Fair to Middling Women,* ancestor of *More Pricks than Kicks.* He'd found it while going through some old papers, he said, and offered to lend it to me if it would interest me. I accepted at once. Then we had a drink and he showed me around the flat and his collection of pictures by Bram van Velde whose work he has admired for many years. When I left, I was not only touched by his extreme kindness and helpfulness, but also elated by the certainty that the mere research student I then was had spent two memorable hours with a great man and one of the leading writers of our time.

After that, I often had occasion to write to Mr. Beckett about this query or that, and he always replied promptly and helped me as much as he could. Between us, I think we have managed to track down the place of first publication of most of his occasional pieces written in the thirties, and in the process several things he had completely forgotten about have come to light. It is always a thrill for me when I come across, in the National Library in Paris or the British Museum, his name or initials at the foot of a piece of writing that has not been noted anywhere before. Sometimes the passage is unsigned, and then I have to ask him whether he wrote it or not.

I had a second meeting with him a couple of years ago. I had sent him a draft list of his works, and we went through it together in the Closerie des Lilas, a favourite haunt of his. We were later joined by Dr. A. J. Leventhal, an old Dublin friend of his who has retired to Paris. Over several glasses of champagne we worked on the list together, and between them they came up with a host of suggestions that have considerably enriched my list. Then we put it aside and talked about more everyday matters. Beckett knew I was due to take up a post in French at Durham University, and asked me if I liked teaching. I said I did, and he told me that he hadn't when he was lecturer at Dublin before Leventhal took over. We talked frankly about people and things, and I derived great pleasure from listening to his soft Dublin accent and watching him laugh. He has a wonderful laugh, and the most remarkable eyes that rivet your attention to his lined, well-constructed features. He inspires immediate sympathy, and only his desire to protect his creative self from hostile prying has given him a reputation for remoteness.

He has had some very kind things to say about what I have written on his work, but we have never discussed my interpretation, or the 'meaning' of his writings. It has always been understood that he could not talk about that, and I have never felt the need to ask him any questions except those that concern bibliographical matters.

Some people may wonder what point there is in digging up an author's every line from obscure journals, and why it is necessary to go to the immense trouble of doing a bibliography on scientific lines, one which gives every detail that the scholar or bibliophile would wish to have, about an author's books and their different editions. I sometimes wonder myself. I think the answer is that bibliography, like lexicography, is the *sine qua non* of accurate and serious literary studies. We take dictionaries for granted; we could not manage without them. In the same way, once an author becomes widely read and studied in schools and universities and homes, as is the case now with Beckett, a good bibliography with accurate dates and data becomes indispensable. So many questions about influence, for instance, can be checked by a glance at a reliable bibliography. Our knowledge of Beckett's changeover to French is deepened when we learn that although his translation of *Murphy* appeared in Paris in 1947, it had, in fact, been completed by the outbreak of war, long before he started writing prose directly in French.

So when our bibliography is published, which I hope will be soon in spite of the work that remains to be done on it, I trust it will be useful. One thing is certain : we could never hope to make it so without Mr. Beckett's assistance.

Although at first I found his books, especially his fiction, very baffling, a theme gradually emerged that helped me to understand them. Thinking it might help others, I wrote my book, *The Novels of Samuel Beckett,* in which I traced the steady decomposition of the Beckettian hero from the Belacqua of *Dream* to the man in the mud of *How It Is,* a breakdown that reflects, and is reflected in, the corruption of the fictional medium. The integrity and selflessness of Beckett's literary odyssey convinced me of his importance, and made me realize that, almost fortuitously, I had chosen to work on one of the great writers of this century.

My work has enabled me to meet several fascinating people, such as Mme Serreau, Mrs. Jolas, and especially his first and greatest director, Roger Blin, who is as kind, and as shy, as Beckett himself, and who has helped me greatly. I only hope that, in my turn, I shall have helped others to an understanding of the works of a great writer and a good man. There the critic's role ends; he can do no more, although he should do no less.

# Waiting for Beckett

ALAN SCHNEIDER

## A Personal Chronicle

*'I take no sides. I am interested in the shape of ideas. There is a wonderful sentence in Augustine: "Do not despair; one of the thieves was saved. Do not presume; one of the thieves was damned." That sentence has a wonderful shape. It is the shape that matters.'*

Samuel Beckett

In the three years that I have come to know him, the shape of Samuel Beckett as a human being has come to matter as much to me as do his plays. Perhaps even more. For Beckett is that most uncompromised of men, one who writes—and lives— as he must, and not as the world—and the world's critics— want him to. An artist, who works with no fears of 'failure', which has fed him most of his writing life, or any expectation of 'success', which has only lately greeted him. A friend, who has come unannounced to see me off at the Gare du Nord although I had not informed him which of the numerous trains to London I might be taking. The head of a physics or math professor set atop the torso and legs of a quarter-miler; a paradoxical combination of a Frenchman's fundamental 'commitment' to life and an Irishman's basic good nature. Such is the shape of the man who has written some of the most terrifying and beautiful prose of the twentieth century.

My first inkling of Beckett's existence came in Zürich,

34

Switzerland, during the summer of 1954. A friend of mine at the Zürich *Schauspielhaus* urged me to look up a new play they had performed the previous season. It was called *Warten Auf Godot,* and its French author had become the rage of intellectual Europe—though, of course, largely unrecognized in his Paris habitat, and unknown in English. When I arrived in Paris a few weeks later, I discovered, after much effect and many blank stares, that *En Attendant Godot* was being presented at an off-beat Left Bank playhouse, the Theatre Babylone. Not quite sure what to expect, my wife and I went the following evening. The theatre was tiny, the production extremely simple. There were nine people in the audience that first evening, a few more when we came again a night later. My French is just good enough to get me in and out of the American Express. Yet through the entire performance I sat alternately spellbound and mystified, knowing something terribly moving was taking place on that stage. When the highly stylized 'moon' suddenly rose and night 'fell' at the end of that first act, I didn't have to understand French in order to react. And when, at the beginning of the second act, the once-bare tree reappeared with little green ribbons for leaves, that simple representation of rebirth affected me beyond all reason. Without knowing exactly what, I knew that I had experienced something unique and significant in modern theatre. *Godot* had me in the beginnings of a grip from which I have never escaped.

The next morning I tried to locate the author to see if the American rights were available. He had no phone, and no one would give me his home address. I left note after note, contacted everyone I could think of who might know—to no avail. Finally a friendly play-agent informed me that the English-language rights had been acquired by a British director Peter Glenville, who was planning to present the play in London with Alec Guiness as Vladimir and Ralph Richardson as Estragon. Besides, added the agent, the play was nothing an American audience would take—unless it could have a couple of top-flight comedians like Bob Hope and Jack Benny kidding it, preferably with Laurel and Hardy in the other two roles.

An American production under those circumstances seemed hopeless, and Mr. Beckett as far removed as Mr. Godot himself. I came home to New York and went on to other matters.

The next spring (1955) I had occasion to remember once more. *Godot* received its English-language première in London, not with Guiness and Richardson at all but with a non-star cast at London's charming Arts Theatre Club. Damned without exception by the daily critics, it was hailed in superlatives by both Harold Hobson and Kenneth Tynan (the Atkinson and Kerr of London) in their Sunday pieces, and soon became the top conversation piece of the English season. At the same time, the English translation was published by Grove Press in New York, and began to sell an extraordinary number of copies not only in New York City but all over the United States. Everyone who could read was beginning to hear about this mysterious *Godot*.

I read and re-read the published version. Somehow, on its closely-spaced printed pages, it seemed cold and abstract, even harsh, after the remarkable ambience I had sensed at the Babylone. When a leading Broadway producer asked me what I thought of its chances, I responded only half-heartedly. Intrigued as I had been, I could not at the moment imagine a commercial production in Broadway terms.

One day in the fall of that same year, I was visiting my old Alma Mater, the University of Wisconsin, when to my utter amazement I received a long-distance phone call from producer Michael Myerberg asking me if I would be interested in directing *Waiting For Godot* in New York. He had Bert Lahr and Tom Ewell signed for the two main roles; and Thornton Wilder, whose *Skin of Our Teeth* I had directed for the Paris Festival that summer, had recommended me. It was like Fate knocking at the door. After a desperate search through practically every bookshop in Chicago, I finally located a copy, stayed up all night on the train studying it with new eyes, and arrived back in New York to breathe a fervent 'yes' to Myerberg.

Followed a series of conferences with Lahr and Ewell, both of whom confessed their complete bewilderment with the play;

36

and with Myerberg, who insisted that no one could possibly be bewildered, least of all himself. He did think it might be a good idea, however, for me to see the English production, perhaps stopping off on the way to have a talk with Beckett himself. To say that I was pleased and excited would be a pale reflection of the reality. And my elation was tempered only by the fear that Beckett would continue to remain aloof—he had merely reluctantly consented to a brief meeting with 'the New York director'.

At any rate, a week later I found myself aboard the U.S.S. *Independence* bound for Paris and London—and, by coincidence, the table companion and fellow conversationalist of Thornton Wilder, who was on his way to Rome and elsewhere. Crossing the Atlantic with Wilder was a stroke of good fortune and an experience I shall never forget. He greatly admired Beckett, considered *Godot* one of the two greatest modern plays (the other was, I believe, Cocteau's *Orpheus*), and openly contributed his ideas about an interpretation of the play, which he had seen produced in both French and German. In fact, so detailed and regular were our daily meetings that a rumour circulated that Wilder was rewriting the script, something which later amused both authors considerably. What was true was that I was led to become increasingly familiar with the script, both in French and in translation, and discovered what were the most important questions to ask Beckett in the limited time we were to have together. More specifically, I was now working in the frame of reference of an actual production situation—a three-week rehearsal period, a 'tryout' in a new theatre in Miami, and, of course, Bert and Tommy. It wasn't Bob Hope and Jack Benny, but that Parisian agent of two summers before had been correct so far. Was she also going to prove correct in terms of the audience response?

Beckett at that time had no phone—in fact, the only change I've noticed in him since his 'success' is the acquisition of one —so I sent him a message by pneumatique from the very plush hotel near the Etoile where Myerberg had lodged me. Within an hour, he rang up saying he'd meet me in the lobby—at the same time reminding me that he had only half an hour or so to spare. Armed with a large bottle of Lacrima Christi, as a present from both Wilder and myself, I stationed myself in the rather overdone lobby and waited for the elusive Mr. Beckett to appear. Promptly and very business-like, he strode in, his tall athletic figure ensconced in a worn shortcoat; bespectacled in old-fashioned steel rims; his face as long and sensitive as a greyhound's. Greetings exchanged, the biggest question became where we might drink our Lacrima Christi; we decided to walk a bit and see if we could come up with a solution. Walk we did, as we have done so many times since, and talk as we walked —about a variety of matters including, occasionally, his play. Eventually, we took a taxi to his skylight apartment in the sixth arrondissement and wound up finishing most of the bottle. In between I plied him with all my studiously-arrived-at questions as well as all the ones that came to me at the moment; and he tried to answer as directly and as honestly as he could. The first one was 'Who or what does Godot mean?' and the answer was immediately forthcoming: 'If I knew, I would have said so in the play.' Sam was perfectly willing to answer any questions of specific meaning or reference, but would not—as always —go into matters of larger or symbolic meanings, preferring his work to speak for itself and letting the supposed 'meanings' fall where they may.

As it turned out, he did have an appointment; so we separated but not before we had made a date for dinner the next evening. On schedule, we had a leisurely meal at one of his favourite restaurants in Montparnasse, then I persuaded him to come along with me to a performance of *Anastasia* at the Theatre Antoine. I had directed the New York production and was interested in seeing what it would be in Paris; it turned out to be very artificial and old-fashioned, and Sam's suffering was acute. Immediately after the last curtain we retired to Fouquet's, once the favourite café of his friend and companion James Joyce, for solace and nourishment. Shortly before dawn —since I had a plane to catch for London—we again separated. But not before Sam had asked me if it would be additionally helpful if he joined me in London at the performances of *Godot* there? He had not been to London in some years, had never

liked it since his early days of poverty and struggle there, but he
would be willing to come if I thought it helpful! I could hardly
believe what I heard. Helpful!

Two days later, Sam came into London incognito, though
some of the London newspapers, hearing rumours of his presence, soon began searching for him. (To this day, he heartily
dislikes interviews, cocktail parties, and all the other public
concomitants of the literary life.) That night, and each night
for the next five days, we went to see the production of *Godot*,
which had been transferred by this time to the Criterion in
Piccadilly Circus. The production was interesting, though
scenically overcluttered and missing many of the points which
Sam had just cleared up for me. My fondest memories are of
Sam's clutching my arm from time to time and in a clearly-
heard stage whisper saying : 'It's ahl wrahng! He's doing it ahl
wrahng!' about a particular bit of stage business or the interpretation of a certain line. Every night after the performance,
we would compare what we had seen to what he had intended,
try to analyse why or how certain points were being lost, speak
with the actors about their difficulties. Every night, also, we
would carefully watch the audience, a portion of which always
left during the show. I always felt that Sam would have been
disappointed if at least a few hadn't.

Through all this, I discovered not only how clear and logical
*Godot* was in its essences, but how human and how easy to know
Sam was, how friendly beneath his basic shyness. I had met
Sam, wanting primarily to latch on to anything which might
help make *Godot* a success on Broadway. I left him, wanting
nothing more than to please him. I came with respect; I left
with a greater measure of devotion than I have ever felt for a
writer whose work I was engaged in translating to the stage.

Though Sam felt he could not face the trials of the rehearsal
and tryout periods, he promised to make his first trip to the
United States once we had opened. As it turned out, he didn't
—and we didn't. Of trials, however, there were plenty, somewhat above the usual quota. Doing *Godot* in Miami was, as
Bert Lahr himself said, like doing *Giselle* in Roseland. Even
though Bert and Tommy each contributed brilliantly comic

and extremely touching performances, even though I felt more or less pleased with the production and felt that Sam would have been equally so, it was—in the words of the trade—a spectacular flop. The opening night audience in Miami, at best not too sophisticated or attuned to this type of material and at worst totally misled by advertising billing the play as 'the laugh sensation of two continents', walked out in droves. And the so-called reviewers not only could not make heads or tails of the play but accused us of pulling some sort of a hoax on them. Although by the second week we were reaching—and holding —a small but devoted audience, the initial reception in Miami discouraged producer Myerberg, demoralized the cast, and led to the abandonment of the production. Later in the season, Myerberg changed his mind and brought *Godot* to Broadway, where it had a critical success; but the only member of the original company to go along was Bert Lahr, who gave substantially the same performance he had given in Miami (but this time without Tom Ewell to match him).

The failure in Miami depressed me more than any experience I had had in the theatre, though I had from time to time anticipated its probability and done all in my power to avoid it. It is typical of Sam that his response to Miami was concerned only with my feelings of disappointment, and never stressed or even mentioned his own. Nor did he utter one word of blame for any mistakes I might have made along the way. Instead he began writing me about his progress on a new play, plans for which he had confided in Paris. He was going to rest for a while at his cottage 'in the Marne Mud' but would try to get to it again as soon as possible.

Somehow, somewhere, I knew I had to make up for Miami —to myself, and more importantly to Sam. I never saw the New York production of *Godot*—perhaps I could not bring myself to—although I have listened over and over again to the recordings. Ostensibly, I was in Europe on a Guggenheim Fellowship, as well as doing some directing in London. By the middle of the summer, I managed to get to Paris and once more face Sam. He made things as bearable as he could for me, and indeed seeing him made them more bearable. We met several

Samuel Beckett at a rehearsal of "Waiting for Godot" at the Royal Court (January 1965) with Anthony Page (left) and Paul Curran (right).

The view from Samuel Beckett's House near the Marne by Henri Hayden.

times. I told him the story of Miami as objectively as I could, and he spoke to me of what he had heard concerning both productions. Somehow he made me feel that what I had at least tried to do in Miami was closer to what he had wanted —though he never criticized the efforts of anyone else. What he made me understand most of all was that he appreciated my concern with his work, that the actual results in Miami didn't matter, that failure in the popular sense was something he had breathed in all his life, and that the only thing which counted was one's own sense of achievement, one's own need to be honest with oneself. No other playwright whom I have ever known could have been so simply and so unselfconsciously unselfish. I would have done anything for Sam.

My opportunity was not long in coming. That new play he was working on was taking shape and had been scheduled for presentation in Paris in the spring of 1957. *Fin De Partie* it was called, again with only four characters (two of them popping out of ashcans) and a special world of its own. The New York press, intrigued by *Godot,* began to publish tidbits about the new play, saying that it was even more 'weird', that it dealt with two men buried up to their necks in wet sand, etc. The title came to be translated as *The End of the Game* and even *The Game Is Up* instead of its proper *Endgame,* as in the last section of a game of chess. Eventually, as it turned out, the French production lost its theatre because of a timid management, and had its première (in French) only through the good offices of the Royal Court in London. Then another management took it over and it ran in Paris through the fall. The London critics, with the exception of Harold Hobson, were even more baffled and negative than they had been with *Godot*; even Tynan confessed his deep disappointment with the newer play's special anatomy of melancholy. While the French critics were, as usual, fervently and hopelessly divided.

Sam had sent me a copy of the French text which I tried, without success, to have someone translate for me. But I didn't have to read every line to know how I felt. One day, I sent him a cable asking for the rights to present the play off-Broadway, where I felt it would reach its proper audience. I had secured the agreement of Noel Behn, manager of the Cherry Lane, one of the best and most intimate of off-Broadway theatres, to present *Endgame* there as soon as its current occupant, Sean O'Casey's *Purple Dust,* had concluded its run; that would probably be around the first of the year. And the reason I wanted to option the play myself was in order to maintain what I felt was a necessary amount of artistic control over all the elements of production, a condition which I had not been able to obtain in my previous encounter with a Beckett play. Fate was knocking at my door for the second time—but this time I was furnishing some of the elbow-grease.

All spring and into the summer I corresponded with Sam and his New York publisher and agent, Barney Rosset of Grove Press, about the arrangements to be made. Although, as Sam said, he felt strange about negotiating for an English translation which did not yet exist. Eventually, after many weeks, it did exist, eventually it came, and eventually—and with a sense of real anticipation—I sat down one evening to read 'the ashcan play', as it had generally become known by this time. In fact, it was only with the greatest of difficulty that we could get the press to understand that the two chief characters were *not* in ashcans.

Though I came to *Endgame* in exactly the opposite manner from which I had been introduced to *Godot,* via the text rather than in the theatre, the experience was equally impressive. Of course, I had come more prepared this time : two years of contact with Sam, a reading and re-reading of all his novels, and of everything I could find that had been written about his work. Whatever the reasons, I found myself literally bowled over by the scope and intensity of the new play's material. Not that I understood everything Sam was driving at; the text was much more taut and elliptical than *Godot's*. But I was certainly carried away with the theatrical powers and possibilities of this alternately terrifying and uproarious, horrible and beautiful, tone-poem. The gentle aged couple in the ashcans was, of course, a marvellous invention and yet completely organic to the theme. But equally fascinating were the two central figures : the blind, majestic, and yet ever-so-human tyrant Hamm, and his shambling automaton attendant Clov. Frankly, I didn't spend much time worrying what all this 'meant' or 'was about —whether it was the last four people left on earth after an atomic explosion; or the older generation being tossed on the ashheap by the younger; or, as someone suggested, Pozzo and Lucky in the third act of *Godot*. Just as *Godot* dealt with a promised arrival that never took place, so *Endgame* dealt with a promised and unfulfilled departure. More than anything else, it seemed to me to be, in a sense, a kind of tragic poem, man's last prayer to a God that might or might not exist. Far from depressing me, it lifted me out of myself, exhilarated me, provided a dramatic experience as strong as the one I had when I first discovered *Oedipus* or *Lear*. And what most delighted me was that in *Endgame* were more of Sam's special gifts for language and rhythm, for making the sublime ridiculous and the ridiculous sublime.

In fact, I wrote to Barney Rosset that the part of Hamm needed a combination Oedipus, Lear, and Hamlet—a neat trick of casting even at Broadway rates, much less off-Broadway. Nevertheless I was determined to try. And, more importantly, Sam was willing to have me try.

With our arrangements for New York production completed, Sam was anxious that I see the Paris version before it closed at the end of October. No more anxious than I. For, once more, I had stored up a fund of questions which could best be answered in person. Luckily, the manager of the Cherry Lane agreed. A trans-Atlantic voyage is a sizeable item in an off-Broadway budget. But in this case a vital one. So in October I was off on my second pilgrimage to Beckett, this time overnight and by air directly to Paris.

As it happened, Sam and I missed each other at the Gare des Invalides on my arrival, but met at the hotel—this time a modest one in Montparnasse (as befitted off-Broadway). For a week we met every day and for most of the day, taking long walks (one lovely sunny afternoon we polished off a pound of grapes while strolling through the Luxembourg Gardens), having lunch and dinner together, inhabiting various cafés at all hours. The French production of *Endgame,* after a run of almost 100 performances, was in its last week; I saw it four times, once while following the English translation with an usher's flashlight until the usher politely told me I was bothering the actors. I spoke with the French cast, especially director Roger Blin, who played Hamm so magnificently; and was able to check on all the technical details of the production. The Paris production had been basically as Sam wanted it, although like all practising playwrights he was gradually discovering that all actors have personalities and get ideas which may seriously affect the intentions of the author. Again Sam tried to answer all my questions, no matter how stupid they seemed to him—or how often I asked them. 'What were Clov's visions?' 'Who was that mysterious Mother Pegg that kept cropping up?' 'What did it mean for Hamm's and Clov's faces to be red, while Nagg's and Nell's were white?' (As Sam counter-asked, why was Werther's coat green? Because the author saw it that way.)

Each time I read the script or saw the play performed, I had a flock of new questions. Sam was always patient and ever tolerant; he wanted to help all he could. And he helped me more than I can ever say or even know. When I left for home, I knew *Endgame* a hundred times better than when I had arrived, knew what Hamm should look like and sound like, knew how best the ashcans should be placed, knew how carefully and how exactly I'd have to work on its rhythms and tones. As for its larger meanings, gradually the mosaic was falling into place, its design still shadowy but perceivable and inevitable.

The main question—contrary to the one I was generally asked : Which play did I like better, *Godot* or *Endgame?*—was : Who in New York could and would play Hamm? In Paris, Blin had given a bravura classic performance in the grand manner, such as only the French theatre could still offer. George Devine, whom I had seen and admired many times, was scheduled to play the role in London; he was excellent casting. What we needed was something of the calibre of Paul Muni—who was seriously ill—or Charles Laughton—who was abroad. I left Paris and Sam's last piece of advice : 'Do it the way you like, Alan, do it ahny way you like!' feeling that somewhere there was bound to be a Hamm—if only we could find him.

Look for him we did! For over two months, the actors streamed in and out of the Cherry Lane offices, and the telephones rang all over New York. Our first choices for the parents were P. J. Kelly and Nydia Westman—and we were fortunate in interesting both. To this day, I can scarcely visualize anyone other than P. J. and Nydia in those ashcans. For Clov, we had several strong choices, depending for our final selection on what kind of Hamm we were to find. Hamm himself remained unobtainable. Muni was indeed not to be had. Laughton wrote us a letter saying he was fascinated by the play but would rather have had Ilse Koch make him into a lampshade than play that part! Others were intrigued but not available, or available but not intrigued; still others interested but somehow not suited. We despaired, postponed, kept looking.

At last, after a brief trial with another actor, we came up with what turned out to be an extremely fortunate choice: a young and relatively unknown performer, Lester Rawlins, with whom I had worked in Washington some years back and who since coming to New York had had his considerable talents hidden behind a succession of Shakespearean beards. For Clov, we took Alvin Epstein, a specialist in mime and the 'Lucky' of the New York *Godot*. (He was later succeeded by Gerald Hiken, not available at the time we were opening, who gave an equally fine performance.) Rawlins had a very low-pitched and flexible voice of great timbre, an imposing presence, and a countenance like granite; at times, he would remind me physically of Blin, yet he succeeded in making the role uniquely and powerfully his own. Epstein's stage movement was always arresting and carefully realized. And Nell and Nagg were adorable. The first hurdle had been well jumped, now we were on our way.

The day after New Year's 1958, we went into rehearsal. First rehearsals of a new play are always a kind of adventure into the unknown, a stepping out into uncharted space. This is especially true of a Beckett play, where so many of the stan-

45

dard conventions are broken or ignored—the beginning, the middle and end of an organized plot-line, clear-cut character progression, dramatic mobility and colour—and yet so many new ones laid down—tones, rhythms, and cross-currents of relationship, which the author has built into the very fibre of his material. No other author I know of writes stage directions which are so essentially and specifically valid—as we discovered to our gain on each occasion when we ventured to disregard or to oppose them. His pauses are as much a part of the text as the words themselves. And I soon found myself not only getting more and more faithful to his printed demands but expecting an equal allegiance from the actors when they tended to go off on their own tangents—as actors are wont to do.

As well as designers. Our setting was being designed by a talented newcomer, David Hays, whose reputation was largely based on his designs for O'Neill's *Long Day's Journey Into Night* and *The Iceman Cometh*. I made the mistake of showing him photographs of the Paris production, whereupon he tried to do everything exactly differently. After he had submitted several designs, all of which were rejected, we discovered that the stone-and-brick walls of the Cherry Lane stage were marvellously available and suited to represent Hamm and Clov's 'shelter'—even to the extent of having a doorway at exactly the proper location for Clov's 'kitchen'. This discovery provided us with a most useful and authentic interior whose actual walls and floor produced sound of great effectiveness, and which could be lit well and simply. How to manage the windows posed our only problem; eventually—and with Sam's wholehearted approval—we painted them, complete with window frames, boldly and theatrically on the wall at the back. (One part of the frame was made practical to allow for its opening near the end of the play.) No one minded in the slightest except those who looked for additional philosophical overtones from two painted windows on a bare brick wall.

Not that we shied away from all 'significance' or meaning. But I have long ago discovered that the director's function is not so much to explain the author's meaning to his actors— whose problem of expressing that meaning to the audience is not necessarily helped by intellectually understanding it—but to see that, through whatever theatrical means, the actors are led to *do* those things which will *result* in the author's meaning being expressed. No actors can act out the *meaning* of *Endgame*—or any other play. They can and did act the roles of the various characters in the various situations and moments and relationships which Beckett had provided for them. They acted them with interest and variety, I hope, and with a sense of form but always as actual people in an actual situation. Beckett himself had always stressed that he was writing about what he termed a 'local situation', i.e., Hamm and Clov (as well as Nagg and Nell) were individual personalities operating in a given set of circumstances. They were not to be considered as abstractions or symbols, or as representing anything other than themselves. After that, if the audience—or the critics— wanted to look for significance of some kind, let them do so, at their own initiative—and peril.

I found, for example, that it became convenient for me to suggest to the actors that the relation of Hamm and Clov could be likened to that of the mind and the body, the intellectual and the physical faculties, inseparable and yet always in conflict. But I never meant that I thought they *were* the mind and the body, or that that was what Sam intended. It was simply a theatrical means of leading the actors into certain areas of creativity and imagination. And definitely more helpful than figuring out whether the names of Hamm and Clov meant ham and cloves, or the Biblical Ham and the cloven foot, and a dozen other secret codes—all of which were obviously irrelevant.

Fortunately, the actors were most co-operative. Nydia Westman, for one, though occasionally or often baffled by what she had to do or say, strove valiantly and with all good will to carry out what I asked her to do. P. J. Kelly, who in his seventy-eight years had had many similar experiences, especially, as he confessed, with Irish playwrights, was equally agreeable. And they both coped good-naturedly with the numerous practical problems involved in making entrances and exits and spending an entire evening in two non-custom-made ashcans. While

47

Rawlins and Epstein, one of whom never left his armchair and the other never allowed to rest from the burden of a constantly uncomfortable stance, did all in their power to carry out their respective jobs as I kept saying—and feeling—Sam would have wanted them to.

By the time we were well into rehearsals, the Cherry Lane management—joined by an optimistic trio known as Rooftop Productions—had no illusions about my initial responsibility being to the author. A number of times during this period, one or the other would get worried that I was making the play 'too serious'. They occasionally urged me to 'gag it up' a bit here and there—which I refused to do, especially since I felt that the production abounded with legitimate laughter. Once or twice, I believe they became upset about one or the other of the performances—or about what I was doing with them. Had I not retained that much coveted artistic control by the very terms of my contract, I might have been forced to make fundamental changes with which I was completely in disagreement—or risked being fired. As it was, I resisted all attempts to change or distort what Sam had written, or go against any of the things he had confided in me during my Paris sojourn and in subsequent letters.

Personally, I felt rehearsals were going extremely well; the texture of Sam's writing was gradually emerging, rich in both its serious and comedic elements. Cast morale was high. Their dedication to the enterprise really remarkable, especially in view of the nominal salaries they were getting and the general lack of glamour of off-Broadway. Interest on the part of the public was also considerable if not tremendous, though we were not getting as much publicity as we wanted. Throughout, I kept constantly in touch with Sam, letting him know all our ups and downs, and continuing to question him in detail—his answers always opening up new vistas and new possibilities.

Three weeks after rehearsals began, we held the first of a series of five previews with audiences. The reception was more than any of us had dared to expect. They laughed and cried at all the proper places, were never bored, though occasionally or even often, puzzled. And not only did they not mind sitting through the hour-and-a-half without intermission (I had refused to add one) but stayed in their seats, clapping wildly at the end. The other four audiences reacted similarly, two or three of them even more enthusiastically. And, miracle of miracles, the word-of-mouth was evidently excellent because we were selling out, an unheard-of event at off-Broadway previews. Advance sales began to hum; the general feeling was that we had a great show. We crossed our fingers and hoped for a good performance on opening night.

Opening night came, and the actors gave the best performance they had yet given. But we found troubles of other sorts. The building's steam pipes had been turned off by accident a half-hour before the curtain went up; and for the first ten minutes, the pipes played a grisly staccato accompaniment to the text that nearly drove me mad and, in my opinion, affected the audience badly. (Afterwards, at least a dozen of my more sophisticated theatre friends told me they thought the sound effects of the pipes were a wonderful touch—though a trifle loud.) In addition, perhaps because the 189-seat Cherry Lane Theatre was more than half occupied by members of the press— something like 100 seats—the audience response was nothing like it had been for the five previews or was going to be for every other night in its run. The audience was respectful but cool. Lines that had brought roars produced hardly a smile, those that had brought smiles produced nothing. Instead of the silences we had previously earned in the more emotional moments of the play, we heard seats creaking and programmes rattling. And opening night was the only night that I didn't hear that on-stage alarm clock ticking from the back of the theatre. We were appalled. And I despaired that all our efforts had again been in vain.

That interval between the curtain coming down on opening night and the first appearance of the reviews in the early editions of the morning papers is a period of purgatory than which nothing in the various hells of the theatre is worse. Somehow we managed to survive its more than ordinary length this time, downing the bourbon and making conversation as though it mattered. A TV commentator at midnight said he had hated

49

us, but we didn't expect anything else from television. At about 12:30, someone from the *Herald-Tribune* rang up and read Walter Kerr's notice directly from the galley sheets. Kerr was respectful if not exactly glowing, somewhat provocative—and there were two or three good quotes. Our spirits, imprisoned since those pipes had started clanking, began to stir. At one o'clock, unable to wait any longer, I rang up the *Times* myself and got a bored voice which after a bit of prodding promised to locate a 'bulldog' edition containing Brooks Atkinson's column. A few interminable moments later, the voice commented 'It's pretty stiff', then having thrown the bomb proceeded to read verbatim an absolutely beautiful notice from Atkinson, one clearly understanding the author's intention and point of view, as well as highly appreciating its representation on the stage. (A few weeks later, Mr. Atkinson came through with an excellent and perceptive Sunday column which added further to our laurels—and our run.) The jubilation was so intense that we couldn't resist letting Sam know. Though it was just dawn in Paris, we telephoned him and told his sleepy self that the two chief critics in New York had liked the production. As usual, Sam's concern was with the performers and the management—though he expressed his gratitude and relief at the favourable reception. The wonderful thing was that I knew, as always, that win, lose, or draw in the notices, Sam's opinion of the entire venture and of me would have been no different. The important thing for him was not the winning or losing of the race but the running of it. I went home for the first time in over two years with the weight of the Miami *Godot* off my shoulders.

Kerr and Atkinson weren't the whole story. As is very usual, the afternoon papers were much more baffled and much less perceptive. But somehow between the word-of-mouth of those who had seen the show and the natural curiosity of those who hadn't, *Endgame* ran three months and more than 100 performances, and was generally regarded as one of the serious highlights of the season on or off Broadway. The weekly press, most of which came the second night, was for the most part good; although we got a bad break when the review in *Time* an extremely favourable one, was crowded out for lack of space. Our audiences grew more receptive and enthusiastic as the run progressed—hardly anyone ever walked out—the performances got fuller and more relaxed, even the publicity improved. But, best of all, we had not failed Sam. Though he would not come to New York to see the production, news and comment about it reached him regularly. He seemed to like the production photographs that had been taken—eventually he will hear the recording of the entire text. Although by then he must have been sure we were able to succeed—as much as any production can. Meanwhile, we continued to look forward to and cherish his occasional 'greetings to the players'.

Beckett's plays stay in the bones. They haunt me sleeping and waking, coming upon me when I am least aware. Sometimes a stray bit of conversation heard by accident on a bus or in a restaurant brings home one of Vladimir's and Estragon's 'little canters'. Sometimes I find myself actually reacting like Clov or like Hamm or, more often, like both simultaneously. Sam's characters seem to me always more alive and more truly lasting than those in the slice-of-life realistic dramas with which our stages today abound. (They will be equally alive when most of those others are as dead as the characters in *The Great Divide*.) His words strike to the very marrow—the sudden sharp anguish of a Pozzo or of a Hamm crying out for understanding in an uncertain universe; Clov's detailed description of the bleak harsh landscape of our existence on earth. While against and in spite of the harshness and the uncertainty, there is the constant assertion of man's will, and spirit, his sense of humour, as the only bulwarks against despair; the constant 'glimmers of hope', even in the dark depths of that abyss in which we find ourselves.

And now Sam has written a new one, actually just a curtain-raiser. For one character and a tape-recorder. *Krapp's Last Tape* it's called, about a man listening to some tapes he has recorded in the past; and as always it manages to be both touching and comedic. His first original writing in English, except for the BBC radio play *All That Fall,* since before the war. An augury? A switch away from French for a while? With

Sam one is never sure. One only hopes that in whatever language, he will go on writing for the theatre because one knows that he will go on extending its boundaries and its dimensions. Not because he plans it that way, but because that is where his taste and imagination and talent lead him.

I shall be content to follow. In fact, I'm on my way over again to see him, a copy of *Krapp's Last Tape* packed in my briefcase. It's getting to be a habit. There are some wonderful sentences in those few pages of *Krapp's Last Tape* as there are in every one of Sam Beckett's plays. I remember especially a group of them near the end : 'Perhaps my best years are gone. When there was a chance of happiness. But I wouldn't want them back. Not with the fire in me now. No, I wouldn't want them back.' Taken together, those sentences leave a wonderful shape. But it is not only their shape that matters. It is the shape of the man who wrote them.

*Reprinted from Chelsea Review, Autumn Number, 1958.*

# PART II

# CRITICAL EXAMINATIONS

# Samuel Beckett's Poems

MARTIN ESSLIN

Of all of Samuel Beckett's writing the slim corpus of his poetry contains his most directly autobiographical utterance. Which is not to say that it yields its secrets easily to all comers. Like a shipwrecked sailor who possesses only a tiny scrap of paper to entrust to the bottle he will fling into the sea and who has to fit the largest possible amount of information about his position into the smallest possible space, Beckett's poems are compressed to the point of being in code : a single line may carry multiple meanings, public and private allusions, description and symbol, topographical reference, snatches of overheard conversations, fragments in other languages, Provençal or German, the poet's own personal asides (like 'main verb at last' at the end of a long sentence in *Sanies I*), learned literary allusions, together with brandnames of cigarettes or shopsigns in Dublin. Four lines may thus require four pages of elucidation, provided that is, that the full information were at hand, could ever be fully elicited.

Yet with the magic of all true poetry, which is mystery, incantation, miraculous pattern of wonder-working words, this poetry compels the reader to read on, to immerse himself and, having entered into the poem, find his way through its internal labyrinth from one revealed fragment of sense to the next glimpse of meaning, until at the centre of the maze a distant vision of the ultimate pattern beckons.

Take, in Beckett's first-published and most self-consciously allusive poem, *Whoroscope,* in which, ostensibly, it is not

55

Beckett who speaks, but Descartes—René du Perron—the lines

> So we drink Him and eat Him
> and the watery Beaune and the stale cubes of Hovis. . . .

Could there be a clearer, a more immediately concrete, sensual image of the Eucharist—with the contrast between the biblical solemnity of the first, the bathetic, descriptive objectivity of the second line, and the added irony of the calculated anachronism (for Beaune might have been marketed in 1650, though I doubt whether under that *appellation controlée*; Hovis most certainly was not)! Ponder those lines and gradually the whole complex structure of the poem will begin to yield its meaning. . . .

Or in *Enueg I* take the image, as the poet reaches Chapelizod on his walk, the lines about

> the Isolde Stores a great perturbation of sweaty heroes
> in their Sunday best,
> come hastening down for a pint of nepenthe or moly or
> half and half
> from watching the hurlers above in Kilmainham. . . .

There is, I am told, a store dispensing drink in Chapelizod called the Isolde Stores (-izod in the place-name being a reference to Iseult, they were so called after the Wagnerian version of that Irish heroine's name). . . . And in the same poem the picture of

> at Parnell Bridge a dying barge
> carrying a cargo of nails and timber. . . .

We were in a broadcasting studio preparing a reading of the poem in Beckett's presence. At this point he asked the reader to put a little more stress on the nails and the timber, which, after all, stood for the cross. So intimately is the descriptive linked with the symbolic in these poems! One is tempted to wonder if the proximity of Parnell's name is not also intentional, as that of another saviour crucified. . . .

Or in the poem entitled *Malacoda,* in which that Dantean

56

monster stands for the undertaker who buried Beckett's father, the description of three stages of the undertaker's appearance in the house—*to measure* the body, *to coffin* it so that it can lie in state, and *to cover* it, coupled with the poet's concern to keep the proceedings from his mother who, at the first stage

> hear she may see she need not

at the second

> hear she must see she need not

while at the third

> hear she must see she must.

In the same poem the lines

> lay this Huysum on the box
> mind the imago it is he

can be made to yield their meaning when one realizes that the Huysum referred to is the Dutch painter Jan van Huysum (1682-1749) who specialized in pictures of flowers and butterflies, reproductions of which were placed on coffins, and that the imago here meant therefore is the butterfly in the picture (larva, pupa and imago being the three stages of insect development) and that imago 'is he'—the dead father, who has emerged from the pupal stage of life into the imago-phase of death (or after-life). Hence the poem ends with the lines:

> all aboard all souls
> half-mast aye aye
> nay

The final nay *denies* the hope of everlasting life after death. And so, incidentally, those five final lines of a poem published by 1935 contain and foreshadow the contents of an entire later novel—*Malone Dies*.

Even more astonishing in its anticipation of the future *argument* of Beckett's complete *oeuvre* to come is the six-line poem *The Vulture* which opens the slim volume *Echo's Bones and Other Precipitates* of which 327 copies were published in 1935.

For this vulture is Death, which drags its hunger through the sky of the poet's skull, that vast internal cavity, that shell which contains the whole world, the sky as well as the earth, that internal universe which also encloses those prone figures of the poet's imagination who will in his future works drag themselves through afflictions of all kind and therefore soon must take up their life and walk, mocked by the tissue of the poet's brain which may not serve as food to the vulture, Death, till that brain itself with all the hunger, all the earth and sky it contains, has died and turned into offal :

> dragging his hunger through the sky
> of my skull shell of sky and earth
>
> stooping to the prone who must
> soon take up their life and walk
>
> mocked by a tissue that may not serve
> till hunger earth and sky be offal

There seems, moreover, in the image of the vulture—and here we have a measure of Beckett's learning, the richness of the store of allusions he can draw on—a definite reference to Goethe's poem *Harzreise im Winter* which opens with the words—

> Like the Vulture
> Who, with feathery wing
> Rests on the morning's
> Heavy cloudbanks,
> Eying his victim,
> Soar up my song. . . .

and which contains this passage about the artist as a lonely outsider who suffers from the isolation and lovelessness of so many Beckett heroes—

> Easy it is to follow the chariot
> Driven by Fortune
> Like the leisurely train
> On mended roads
> Of a Prince's progress.

58

But who is it that stands
Apart?
His path is lost in the thicket
Behind him the bushes
Close up,
The grass stands again
Deserts engulf him.

Oh who heals the sorrow
Of him, whose balm turned to poison?
Who drank misanthropy
Out of love's flood?

Beckett's poem about the vulture consists of no more than six lines. Yet these six lines open up, through allusion, a vast treasure-house of the past, while, at the same time forecasting all of Beckett's writing which was yet to come.

peering out of my deadlight looking for another
wandering like me eddying far from all the living
in a convulsive space
among the voices voiceless
that throng my hiddenness

These lines from a poem (originally written in French) dated 1948 echo not only Beckett's own verses of *The Vulture* itself, but Goethe's also. The original French text sums up Beckett's narrative writings even more clearly:

dans un espace pantin
sans voix parmi les voix
enfermées avec moi

It is in Beckett's plays, stories and novels that we hear those voices that are enclosed within the world of his skull tell the stories of those prone figures who must take up their life and walk. In his *poems,* however, we briefly hear the voice of Samuel Beckett himself. He may argue, and indeed is almost certain to argue, that those voices spring from deeper levels of experience, that the Self which we glimpse walking through Dublin, London and Paris, over Parnell Bridge and through

Regents Park or the Rue Mouffetard, is a more superficial, external Self than that which finds expression in the unceasing drone of those voices. And while we must inevitably agree with this view and accept that, once those voices had begun to speak loudly and clearly, the private, personal and more external poetry had to cease, we cannot but treasure Beckett's poems for the glimpses they give us of the rare, ascetic and saintly personality from which those voices issued forth.

And indeed, all of Beckett's writing is ultimately poetry, if poetry be defined as a structure of language in which the manner of the saying is of equal importance with the matter that is said, in which indeed the manner of saying and the matter said completely and organically coincide. In that sense Beckett's prose and plays also are poetry : structures of words so intricately, so delicately balanced that the removal of a single one would cause the whole edifice to lose its symmetry.

When the voices asserted their right to speak, Beckett himself stopped writing verse. But occasionally the voices themselves speak in verse. And that verse is as concise, as economical, as profound and essential as Beckett's personal poetry. Can there be a more memorable summing up of that basic image of all of Beckett's oeuvre, the final equation of *Birth* into a world unfathomable to the frightened being on the threshold of life, and *Death,* that terrified emergence into another unfathomable, unknowable state of being, than the final poem composed by the voice called Words in *Words and Music*?

> Then down a little way
> Through the trash
> Towards where
> All dark no begging
> No giving no words
> No sense no need
> Through the scum
> Down a little way
> To whence one glimpse
> Of that wellhead.

# *Progress Report,* 1962-65

HUGH KENNER

Beckett's way of making progress is like that of the man in *How It Is*—'ten yards fifteen yards semi-side left right leg right arm push pull flat on face imprecations no sound'— varying nothing except the programme of the mute imprecations and dragging after him everything he has had since he started. That is why, as his works multiply, their resemblances become more and more striking, for their components, it grows increasingly clear, are drawn from a limited set. It is also why their originality of convention grows more and more absolute, for invention consists in devising new sets of rules by which the familiar pieces may be chosen and shown. To play one more game by the old rules would merely be competence, and a new medium (film, television) is a great liberator of invention. Inspecting, therefore, the stage plays since *Endgame* (*Happy Days* and *Play*) or the radio plays since *Embers* (*Words and Music* and *Cascando*), or the film (*Film*) or the TV play (*Eh Joe*), or even the fictional fragment (*Imagination Dead Imagine*), we sense with equal accuracy that we have seen all their elements before, and that the author nevertheless is repeating nothing. And one last little play, the 'dramaticule' *Come and Go,* in evading most of the familiar Beckett rituals contrives to be the most characteristic of all.

All these works are mysteriously situated, in that never-world which is perhaps the interior of the author's head, or the auditor's. Their action (except for that of *Come and Go*) proceeds at the bidding of some mysterious authority which resembles Murphy's 'process of supernatural determination', so that the figures before us perform but do not design their performance. This authority is itself one of the figures before us, in the acoustical space of the radio plays where it is so difficult to give a meaning to 'before us' : the inciting croaking voice in *Words and Music,* the voice of the 'Opener' ('dry as dust' but frantic later) in *Cascando.* In the visual works, betrayed by no tremor because inaudible, it expresses its will more austerely, the eye's being the rhetoric of tyranny as the ear's of misgivings. It distils the authority of the very medium : the TV camera itself, the ciné camera itself. In *Play* it directs the inquisitorial spotlight, in *Happy Days* it rings 'the bell for waking and the bell for sleep'.

These bells, according to the convention of *Happy Days,* are indispensable, daylight being now eternal. Yet being rung by somebody, they mechanize what remains vestigially a voice. They cannot counterfeit the indifference with which a turning earth's daylight comes and goes. If Winnie does not at once begin her day, the waking bell rings again, 'more piercingly'. 'Someone is looking at me still,' she reflects as its echoes die out. 'Caring for me still. (*Pause.*) That is what I find so wonderful. (*Pause.*) Eyes on my eyes. (*Pause.*)' If she knew she was in a theatre we might suppose she was speaking of the audience, whose presence exacts her performance, and thanks to whose interest the run of the play continues, as she sinks deeper into the rote of her part, gesturing at last with nothing more than her eyes. It is like Beckett to contrive as bleak a play as possible, and then toy with the fancy of its running interminably; equally like him to work so close to the nerve of the form that we cannot tell whether our own remorseless curiosity is part of the play or not. Perhaps it is not; the bell, though it synchronizes with our impatience, would be rung by the stage electrician with equal rigour were the opening-night house empty. It resembles in this way the will of God, which commands the private as surely as the public self. The importunate flicking spotlight that conducts the human orchestra of *Play* is in the same way both a metaphor for our attention (relentless, all-consuming, whimsical) and a force within the play which *directs* our attention, and on which we rely for direction, as movie-goers rely on the camera. A play is an inquisition at which we connive. Once it has ceased to be, like the *Oresteia* or even *Richard II,* a public ritual religious in context, it transforms itself into a low ritual of curiosity, the symbols of which are not the hero and his fate, but the curtain, the cues, the lights. The drama of Ibsen and his successors celebrates our conviction that we have a right to *find out.* Blending deceptively with the known world, it reduces the known world, people and all, to the plane where specimens are studied.

*Endgame* is Beckett's one homage to the drama of Sophocles and Shakespeare : an X-ray version of the heroic play, dominated by Hamm, a prince of players. Its predecessor, *Waiting for Godot,* reflects something more primitive : the intercourse of clowns, before the arrival of a hero who does not arrive. *Happy Days,* with its plethora of domestic detail, is post-heroic : tooth-brush, lipstick, shopping-bag, parasol, and a great fat heroine who sings and smiles and quotes and projects her battered personality : her things are the bric-à-brac and hers the rituals of an English music-hall 'turn', circa 1890. Already the compassion of the audience contains latent cruelties; the famous Marie Lloyd, like Beckett's Winnie, had perpetually to demean herself, more than any male clown, as a condition of her habitual moral triumph. And *Play,* finally, is School of Ibsen : incomparably the least 'realistic' even of Beckett's plays, yet more closely entangled than any in mundane tensions (husband, wife, mistress), and more cruelly compliant to the rigours of an audience that will not be appeased until it has known, vicariously, every humiliation these three can inflict on one another. What the audience receives and accepts is of course finely enamelled cliché :

> Judge then of my astoundment when one fine morning, as I was sitting stricken in the morning room, he slunk in, fell on his knees before me, buried his face in my lap and . . . confessed.

This language smoothly parodies itself : 'as I was sitting stricken in the morning room.' (Does anyone outside of plays ever *speak* the word 'stricken'? How does one go about the ritual of 'sitting stricken'? And are we to suppose that the morning room is the specially appointed locale for this piece of business?) Yet it is the parody, the fine enamel Beckett applies to his clichés, that makes the doings believable and bearable: we will insist on blood, but we will be satisfied only by formulae.

As *Play* moves on from Beckett's earlier plays ('Call that moving,' said The Unnamable; 'Call that on'), so it recapitulates also certain effects developed in the drama for radio. Its three persons (though it is true we can see them) have no names and do nothing but speak, on cue. *Embers* had carried to a seeming limit the major premise of broadcast drama, that it is an affair of voices in a dark world. *Words and Music* pushes this limit back.

> MUSIC: *Small orchestra softly tuning up.*
> WORDS: Please! (*Tuning. Louder.*) Please! (*Tuning dies away.*) How much longer cooped up here, in the dark? (*With loathing.*) With you! (*Pause.*)

These are the play's opening seconds, and here are the two irreducible conventions of radio, the music and the voice, holding exacerbated dialogue in the dark. Like the bells in *Happy Days,* they have persons attached to them. 'Rap of baton on stand' makes it clear that Music is something more than a collective sonorousness, and Words has not only a voice but a set of frayed nerves. Having gotten Music to be quiet, he proceeds to intone an analytic passage on his most congenial passion, which happens to be the anti-passion, sloth. He is not reciting this, either, but composing it, as the missteps and revisions indicate, and we shall later find Music as well engaged in acts of composition.

An imprisoned belletrist, then, and an imprisoned musician, 'here in the dark'; they are named, we learn, Joe and Bob; and their master, addressed by no name and designated in the script as 'Croak', calls them 'my comforts' and implores them, more than once, to be friends. This master can get about; he arrives and leaves on shuffling carpet slippers; he descends from a tower, plagued on the stairs by the apparition of a face; he calls his 'comforts' to order with the thump of a club. All this is eerie melodrama, calmly posited, as preposterous as the melodrama of the Shelter in *Endgame*; are Words and Music perhaps faculties immured in Croak's brain, as Hamm, Clov, Nagg and Nell occupied a room like the interior of an immense skull? They perform at his bidding, indeed compose in anguish at his bidding, to themes of his announcing. He announces, in succession, three themes: (1) Love, (2) Age ('old age I mean,' falters Words, 'if that is what my Lord means,' and his Lord does not contradict him), and (3) The Face. On Love they expatiate in succession, quarrelling and with little conviction; Words, indeed, simply refurbishes for the occasion his private monologue on Sloth. On Age, with immense reluctance but implacably commanded, they work up a song, revising as they go, feeling their way, Music generally leading; and the horror of Age, this song will have us know, is when

> She comes in the ashes
> Who loved could not be won
> Or won not loved . . .

My Lord's croaking voice next specifies the third theme:

CROAK: (*murmur*). The face. (*Pause.*) The face. (*Pause.*) The face. (*Pause.*) The face.

This, we are to understand, is the face that haunts him on the tower stairs, and detains him and shakes his will; and Words commences to describe how such a face looks when, apparently reclining, it is seen from above, and by starlight.

> Seen from above at such close quarters in that radiance so cold and faint with eyes so dimmed by . . . what had passed, its quite . . . piercing beauty is a little . . .

[Here some interruptions, after which the voice resumes]

> . . . blunted. Some moments later, however, such are the powers of recuperation at this age, the head is drawn

back to a distance of two or three feet, the eyes widen to a stare and begin to feast again. (*Pause.*) What is then seen would have been better seen in the light of day, that is incontestable.

He proceeds to a frigid inventory of attributes :

—flare of the black disordered hair as though spread wide on water, the brows knotted in a groove suggesting pain but simply concentration more likely all things considered on some consummate inner process, the eyes of course closed in keeping with this, the lashes. . . .

It is the familiar Beckett discipline of the specifying phrase and the declarative sentence, bathetic in its pedantry yet heroically right in preferring pedantry to speechless misery. For this is Croak's vanished love, articulated for him by Words in a passage curiously like that reminiscence of passion in a slowly drifting boat which comes back from Krapp's tape again and again ('We lay there without moving. But under us all moved, and moved us, gently, up and down, and from side to side.') Stoically the inventory proceeds downward, hair, brows, eyes, nose, lips, breasts; it is like a Renaissance catalogue of charms, drily paraphrased. Then her face grows suddenly animated, like a reviving Juliet's; 'then down a little way . . .'

Here pedantry surrenders; poetry supervenes; and, Music aiding, the language gropes toward a grey epithalamion.

It is instructive to observe a refusal of pedantry to surrender, in what reads like the gist of a Science-fiction novel, the thousand-word *Imagination Dead Imagine*. Here an observer, attentive to cycles of light, of temperature, of occulted eyes, scrutinizes amid a lunar whiteness a recumbent couple crammed into a vaulted circle :

Still on the ground, bent in three, the head against the wall at B, the arse against the wall at A, the knees against the wall between B and C, the feet against the wall between C and A, that is to say inscribed in the semicircle ACB, merging in the white ground were it not for the

66

long hair of strangely imperfect whiteness, the white body of a woman finally.

That is his tone, that remains scrupulously his tone, as he examines signs of life ('Hold a mirror to their lips, it mists') or notes 'the left eyes which at incalculable intervals suddenly open wide and gaze in unblinking exposure long beyond what is humanly possible. . . . Never the two gazes together except once, when the beginning of one overlapped the end of the other, for about ten seconds.' They do not gaze into each other's eyes, they lie back to back. And having murmured 'ah, no more' and left them he reflects that there is no other life anywhere and no hope of locating these two again :

> . . . no question now of ever finding again that white speck lost in whiteness, to see if they still lie still in the stress of that storm, or of a worse storm, or in the black dark for good, or the great whiteness unchanging, and if not what they are doing.

Croak yields to no such sterility of feeling; he has Words and Music compose him a dismal, gratifying song. To rehearse in the mind, in time of need, the gratifications life never offered, or, offering, saw refused : this is Croak's need and Croak's comfort. It transcends the sexual; it restates Bolton's unspecifiable need for Holloway ('Please! Please!'), and only art or something like art, in this solipsist's nightmare world of dungeons and haunted towers, can make a show of allaying it now. Bolton and Holloway, in the story Henry in *Embers* tells himself, enact repeatedly the need for communion which Henry had denied in his rejection of his wife. Words and Music similarly, though unlike Bolton and Holloway in being faculties rather than puppets, gratify Croak with the ritual articulation of a comparable need. The narrator of *Imagination Dead Imagine* gratifies himself with the chill impossibility of articulating it, of articulating anything but quantifiable fact.

In another radio piece, *Cascando,* a nameless 'Opener' also surrenders to need, a Voice and a melodic line again responding. Here things are more austere; there is no hint of Gothic décor, no 'Joe' and 'Bob', no club, no quarrelling: only the ceremonious 'I open', and in response the prompt obedient Voice:

> story ... if you could finish it ... you could rest ... you could sleep ... not before ... oh I know ... the ones I've finished ... thousands and one ... all I ever did ... in my life ... with my life ... saying to myself ... finish this one ... it's the right one ... then rest ...

It is the voice in which Malone, The Unnamable, Hamm and Henry have told in their time stories to themselves, groping towards repose; it presses on, 'low, panting', to limn yet another Beckett vagrant, called Woburn this time; it follows him, as he refuses the hills and presses out to sea; and it is under the unquestionable control of Opener, who can quell it with another ceremonious phrase: 'And I close.' He can open Music too, and close Music; and he can command Voice and Music to perform in concert, and command them to cease. So with his repertory of openings and closings he directs this strange performance. Voice sketching the shambling tale, Music intervening or sustaining on command, Woburn (in the story) stumbling onto the shingle, collapsing (like the hero of *La Fin*) into a boat, committing himself to the waves.

But the air of steely control is an illusion; Opener protests from time to time a suspiciously Stoical indifference to what 'they' say.

> They say, that is not his life, he does not live on that. They don't see me, they don't see what my life is, they don't see what I live on, and they say, That is not his life, he does not live on that.
>
> *Pause.*
> I have lived on it ... pretty long.
> Long enough.
> Listen.

He presses forward with his performance, opening and closing the vocal and instrumental parts, crying as though nearing a climax, 'Come on! Come on!' This will be (if he can catch up with Woburn, 'see him ... say him') the last story, that brings peace; and then Voice or Music suddenly flags into silence his consternation is terrible: 'Good God good God.' He flogs his flagging powers:

> don't let go ... finish ... it's the right one ... I have it ... this time ... we're there ... Woburn ... nearly—

Yet no more than an act of onanism can the pursuit of Woburn bring communion, and the frenzied music and frenzied words,

> ... we're there ... nearly ... just a few more ... don't let go ... Woburn ... he clings on ... come on ... come on—

lapse into a terminal stage direction:

*Silence.*

In *Film* an implacable hunting down is prosecuted, subject to no failure of nerve or of resource because conducted by a machine, the camera; conducted, therefore, on behalf of ourselves, the spectators, who have (have we not?) the *right*. For the camera is our deputy; we look as it looks, moves, pries, pursues, incited by our lust to see the face of a man who does not allow his face to be seen. This man (played by Buster Keaton) 'storms along in comic foundered precipitancy', through the street, up the stairs, to his room, followed by a camera (ourselves) which is surprisingly careful to spare him 'the anguish of perceivedness': for on two occasions when a glimpse of his face is almost caught it is the camera, not he, that draws back. The camera is less sparing of other faces; once 'an elderly couple of shabby genteel aspect' undergoes its scrutiny, and once a frail old flower-woman. The couple is transfixed with horror and hastens away, though its pet monkey is indifferent; apparently 'the anguish of perceivedness' is reserved for humans. The flower-woman 'closes her eyes, then sinks to the ground and lies with her face in scattered flowers'. These people it withers, acutely looking at them, as in the screening-room the Argus-eyed audience acutely looks at them; but until the last implacable confrontation it spares the anonymous 'O'. (The script calls him O, for Object; the camera is E, for Eye.)

Followed by this intermittently compassionate Eye from the great world (street) through the little world (stairs) to the littlest world (the room), O proceeds to eject or occlude a little universe of Eyes. Window is curtained, mirror covered; dog and cat ('large cat and small dog; unreal quality') are expelled, a ritual requiring seventeen subroutines, each beast repeatedly re-entering as he expels the other; the face of God the Father with staring eyes is ripped from the wall and torn in four; the unblinking eye of a parrot and the magnified eye of a goldfish are in turn occulted by an overcoat.

There remains, as for Croak, the past : here a kind of film within the film, as so often in Beckett's work the play within the play or the story within the story; for a film is a blended sequence of stills, and O deals next with seven photographs, his life-story, dealt out one by one as in a time-lapse scrutiny of a flower unfolding. Each features eyes; his mother's 'severe eyes devouring' him in infancy, his dog looking up at him, his infant daughter looking into his face, 'exploring it with finger'. Only in the seventh picture ('30 years. Looking over 40') is he quite alone; his expression is grim; and his own left eye is covered with a patch. This last picture he destroys, and he then proceeds to destroy each of the others in reverse order, consuming his past as he moves backward through it. (The infant is tough to obliterate; heavier cardboard perhaps.) And now he is alone.

But not alone. The camera waits. It circles him as he sleeps; it fixes his face at last ('patch over left eye'); its gaze awakens him; they exchange gazes; and finally we are shown *it*. And it has his face. It is ourselves? It is an aspect of himself. 'It is O's face (with patch), but with very different expression, impossible to describe, neither severity nor benignity, but rather acute *intentness*. A big nail is visible near left temple (patch side). Long image of the unblinking gaze.' Being a

70

camera, it is monocular and does not blink. Being the suffering O, it bears a nail (it is also a cinematic denizen, so we are not wrong to be reminded of Frankenstein's monster). Being intent, it is ourselves. The film is about us, and the selves we go to the cinema to hunt and scrutinize. And it is about the self-scrutiny, the agonizing ultimate confrontation no Beckett being can evade. What Krapp confronted listening to his past, what Croak transmuted into commissioned song and Opener into Woburn (though Woburn evades him), what the chill notation of *Imagination Dead Imagine* encapsulates into cold friction and jettisons, O must stare at, we must stare at. 'Search of non-being in flight from extraneous perception breaking down in inescapability of self-perception,' runs the script's initial summary of *Film*. And a circle long left open closes; for the final confrontation with the Self occurs in just such a rocking-chair as Murphy, long ago, had taken for the magic cradle of his ritual rock into Nirvana.

In another work another mechanism is equally implacable. The television camera fixes a man named Joe, indeed locks his head into a box in the spectator's living room and holds it there to expand slowly in terror as a toneless voice, a woman's, stabs him with reminiscent phrases. 'Thought of everything?' she begins, for he has just closed the window and locked the door and closet, and not omitted to glance under the bed. Is he afraid some bedbug will see him, she asks. It is not bedbugs he fears, as he sits on that bed, but just such memories as her voice brings, and just such self-knowledge : memories that invade the air and fill his motionless head, and are not to be ripped in four as O ripped the photographs. 'Eh Joe,' she repeats, 'Eh Joe ... Eh Joe ...', insidiously intimate as he and she were once intimate; and the tale she tells of suicide, of a girl (she says not herself; there have been many girls) who tried with water and knife and finally managed with pills, to be found by the sea with her head pillowed on the stones, perhaps explicates Joe's plight; for he had certainly appreciated this girl, whose post-coital gaze was 'unique in his experience', but not appreciated her sufficiently for her not to choose not to live.

71

Work after work rings changes on this inquisitorial theme. In *Play* (a title which means that someone or something is playing) the Croak of one radio drama, the Opener of another, the camera of Film, the off-camera voice of *Eh Joe,* becomes a spotlight, flicking to and fro across three immobile faces, and soliciting their speech at its whim. It is quite calm, but it will never learn anything new. This light, in a way the chief character, has none of Croak's pathos nor Opener's frenzy; nameless like them, it is voiceless also, more so even than Winnie's minatory bell. It does not participate in the three people's gone passion; no spotlight could. It extracts their story; they are human and other, subject not even to its curiosity but to its mere inquisitorial ritual; and it presses toward no climax but merely toward the moment to begin again, and after that again, having all eternity to play in. The curiosity is wholly ours.

For this is a cunning work, which grants the audience every needful opportunity including the opportunity to hear the whole thing twice. In mid-career it commences to repeat itself exactly,\* and completes the repetition down to the man's terminal question, 'Am I as much as ... being seen?' It then commences a third repetition. We need the recapitulation, as of a film being reshown or a record being replayed, so we can be quite sure what is happening, or what has happened. The play, moreover, needs the recapitulation too, by way of establishing its norm of utterly mechanical recollection in eternal tranquillity, as though some cosmic Krapp were intercutting three tapes forever, condemned indeed to intercut them forever, and according to unvarying formulae : for it is very odd that not only do the voices speak the same speeches in the same order, but the spotlight solicits them unfailingly in the same order too, and accords each fragment of each speech the same

---

\* This account follows the published text throughout. In directing the 1964 London and Paris performances, Beckett virtually improvised a new work (*Play No. 2* ?) by modifying the rigour of the light. It grew tired; it faded (and the voices with it); it relaxed its rigorous sequence for soliciting speeches. Perhaps it would eventually go out and release the players into non-being; or perhaps it was teasing them with this hope. When he prepared the French text for publication (*Comédie*, 1966), Beckett did not however incorporate these revisions, though he outlined them in a note as an alternative mode of performance.

duration as the first time, before cutting it off at the same word. Some destiny guides that light, or guides the destiny that guides the light, in a hell of infinite regress. The second half of *Happy Days,* like the second half of *Molloy* or the second half of *Waiting for Godot,* suggests a repetition of the first, though with the slight changes that attend any attempt at repetition in a universe subject to change and entropy. The second half of *Play* is (except for its effect on our minds) identical with the first half of *Play,* in a machine-universe immune from time, change, experience, memory, or communion.

None of the three inhabitants, in this artifice of eternity, knows the other two are there. They are fixed to the chin in huge white urns, 'faces so lost to age and aspect as to seem almost part of the urns'. They have each of them a perfectly connected story, recited with interruption but without hiatus; skipping down the printed script, we can read each version through as though the others were not there. Like tapes switched on and off, they seem not to know, until halfway through each cycle, that they are being stopped and started; they merely resume and lapse. They are as nameless as the light that cues them.

Each time round, though, the cycle breaks at mid-point as the three of them, their narratives ended, commence bitterly to resent the flicking light. 'Hellish half-light,' says the wife. 'Get off me! Get off me! . . . Is it that I do not tell the truth, is that it, that some day somehow I may tell the truth at last and then no more light at last, for the truth?' Here is the familiar Beckett ordeal, trying to tell the right story so as to be permitted peace; but each time round she tells the same story, syllable for syllable. The mistress, on the other hand, is tormented by no fierce ideal of truth; she merely supposes (and rather hopes) that the light is driving her out of her wits, and will tire of her when or before it succeeds. Each of them supposes that while she suffers the other lives on, up in the daylight, with the man. As for the man, he knows that he is dead, for he had chosen death. Death is not the peace he had expected, in which 'all that pain' would be 'as if . . . never been'.

'It will come. Must come. There is no future in this.' He has now revalued, at least, the life in the sun. 'I know now, all that was just . . . play. And all this? When will all this— . . . all this, when will all this have been . . . just play?' For the future's role is to reduce the sharp past to 'just play': if only it were possible to suppose that ahead of this state lies a future.

What is this state? For him, apparently, death. For them, inquisition, perhaps self-inquisition, whether alive or dead. It is a little as though, after his disappearance, the two women in his life were undergoing a merciless third-degree, whether self-inflicted, or inflicted by officials, or inflicted by the justice that presides over some ante-chamber of hell. They have all three entered, at any rate, the world of *The Unnamable,* or *How It Is,* where a sunlit life is remembered in fragments; though how people enter this world they never know. They need not know. They are in it. Dante's Belacqua was condemned to dream through again, for as long as he had passed on earth, his life on earth, and Beckett's Murphy, amateur of the 'Belacqua bliss', rather cherished the notion of such a post-mortem respite on the threshold of the vigours of heaven. But if life on earth, redreamed, comes to be justly valued as 'just play', the act of redreaming it does not. 'No doubt I make the same mistake as when it was the sun that shone,' says the mistress, 'of looking for sense where possibly there is none.' And a moment later, 'Are you listening to me? Is anyone listening to me? Is anyone looking at me? Is anyone bothering about me at all?'

The audience, of course, is looking and listening: it is the ultimate inquisitor. For Beckett has once again carefully doubled with his play the fact that it is a play, that the actors must repeat it over and over as long as there are spectators who will come, and that those spectators are possessed by a rage to find out: a rage exacerbated by the bizarre surface the author has imparted to this entertainment. The very impediments which his intercutting puts in the way of our finding out what has gone on summon from us an irritated intentness which the work in turn makes use of. *Play* is everything that happens inside the theatre, which contains considerably more viewers than actors. And the actors have learned their parts, are letter-perfect in their parts. The viewers have not.

So we strain our attention, and what we find out is soon told. The man was having an affair. His wife accused him, and accused his mistress. Since she had no proof, these accusations had a certain comic edge, not lost on the mistress at least: rage is always tasteless, and the tasteless bizarre ('What are you talking about, I said, stitching away. Someone yours? Give up whom? I smell you off him, she screamed. He stinks of bitch.'). The wife has lost, if she ever had it, whatever sense warns people that they are quoting bad plays. She threatens her own life, threatens the life of the mistress, and even engages a detective. The husband, alarmed by these threats of mayhem, placates each woman by swearing to give up the other. He gives up neither, of course. Eventually he can sustain the double life no longer, and disappears, apparently into death. Perhaps after that the wife carried out her threats; at any rate, they are all three now side by side in the urns.

On earth they were play-acting, sustained by clichés of language and action. Here is the mistress:

> She came in again. Just strolled in. All honey. Licking her lips. Poor thing. I was doing my nails, by the open window. He has told me all about it, she said. Who he, I said, filing away, and what it? I know what torture you must be going through, she said, and I have come to say I bear you no ill-feeling. I rang for Arsene.

That is preposterous: the one's compassion, the other's coldness, each speaking in pastiche. Here is the husband:

> At home all heart-to-heart, new leaf and bygones bygones. I ran into your ex-doxy, she said one night, on the pillow, you're well out of that. Rather uncalled-for, I thought. I am indeed, sweetheart, I said, I am indeed. God what vermin women. Thanks to you, angel, I said.

That life was was indeed 'all play'. They assembled its details out of plays. And now their play, their *jeu de mots*, is indelible. Down in the very rhythm of the sentences, where style assem-

75

bles well-smoothed epithets compactly, lurks the grotesque falseness which was all any of them could ever really articulate, and which, reciting facts over and over again, they are now condemned to rearticulate forever. That is what they were storing up, all those years, in the famous vessels in which Beckett in *Proust* imagined the finest moments of the past being sealed away: the vessels out of which the voices now come. Theirs is not what the protagonist of 'Dante and the Lobster' called ('God help us all') a quick death. There is no quick death, in this Irish post-Protestant world of afterworld. The light too is deathless.

An inquisitor, generally not human; and a past to resuffer, transmute, or destroy: permuting these elements through several media Beckett has made this brilliant sequence of minor works: wrenching, rigorous, ghastly, his great comic gift subsumed into grim precisions of style that render the inquisition ever more refractory. But if we suppose he has boxed himself up we are mistaken, for the little three-minute coda *Come and Go* dispenses with inquisition and obsessive suffering. Its mode is tactful compassion; its agonies, barely touched, perhaps for the future. These women come and go not in a room but silently, on rubber soles, in and out of a circle of light, and they talk not of Michaelangelo but in tactful whispers of one another's apparent infirmities. Their age is 'undeterminable'. Their first words suggest the witches in *Macbeth*: 'When did we three last meet?' (The reply is 'Let us not speak.') A few lines later they are three little maids from school: 'Just sit together as we used to, in the playground at Miss Wade's.' Between that time and the present they have undergone the damage of a lifetime, and there may be worse to come; as each in turn leaves briefly the other two exchange variants of the same dialogue:

FLO : Ru.
RU : Yes.
FLO : What do you think of Vi?
RU : I see little change. (*Flo moves to central seat, whispers in Ru's ear. Appalled.*) Oh! (*They look at each*

76

*other. Flo puts her finger to her lips.*) Does she not
realize?

FLO : God grant not.

Each has this sort of secret to tell of one other; each, having
taken part in two such dialogues, perhaps guesses what is
being withheld from her, or perhaps does not guess (how
powerful is the argument from analogy? How powerful is
willed illusion?) And they hold hands, 'Dreaming of . . . love',
explicitly not speaking of 'the old days', or 'of what came
after', but thinking they feel on one another's fingers the rings
no one can see. Three lives are telescoped into three minutes,
in a vignette so spare that each of just 121 spoken words is
shaped by dozens of words not spoken. Suffused in their disappointment, sustained by their wistful re-enactment, braced
by their interlinked connivance to withhold from one another
intelligence of rumoured agonies, they make of their reticence
their lifetime's finest achievement; and Beckett has very nearly
made a play out of silence.

# PART III

# TRIBUTES

# Beckett the Magnificant

MADELEINE RENAUD

Before playing *Oh! Les Beaux Jours* (*Happy Days*) I liked
Beckett's work, and ever since I have admired the man, although he intimidates me.

First of all, he is very handsome, with a fascinating charm
of which it seems to me he is unaware. And then, naturally,
he is intelligent and subtle, possessing a rare tact and courtesy.
When he came to Paris for rehearsals, he asked me : 'Would
it upset you if I helped you with your part?' Usually authors
insist on it, and they are right to do so.

For two months Roger Blin, Beckett and I worked together
in the empty, silent halls of the Odéon. We learned every
word by heart, every speech in the most absolute confidence.
Yes, Beckett showed complete confidence in Roger Blin and
myself. He was always there, terribly present and yet silent.
Once, when a certain passage was giving me trouble, he said
to me : 'But, if it worries you, it must be cut!' Coming from
an author, it was a very rare phrase indeed. And as he possesses a sense of theatre to an astonishing degree, the sense of
creating an effect, we also accorded him an equal confidence.

I can say that those two months of rehearsal were very rich
for me. First of all as an actress—I have a long career behind
me, and yet Blin and Beckett opened a completely new window onto my career. And then too as a woman. Certainly
my contacts with Beckett were difficult : he speaks very little,
never makes confidences, never allows himself to be taken by
surprise; he only reveals himself through his writings; and he
never comes to performances of his plays because he cannot

bear to find himself in direct contact with the public. Does this mean that he despises them? I do not think so, but rather that he suffers from extreme embarrassment.

Who knows Beckett? Undoubtedly his wife does. But as for others, for myself? I only know what he looks like.

We worked together for two months, in total confidence; he came to dinner several times at my house, and it was certainly not from a desire to be social. But I have never been to where he lives and I do not possess any photograph of him. From time to time he sends me a card. That is all.

But all the same, I know that he thinks of me as a friend and that this friendship is loyal; I have the proof of it. A film director (why not name him, it was Jean-Luc Godard) asked him for permission to film *Oh! Les Beaux Jours*. Beckett refused and replied that he could not envisage *Oh! Les Beaux Jours* without Madeleine Renaud. Authors, where their interest is concerned, do not often feel themselves committed to their interpreters to this extent. But Beckett is more than an author, he is a poet. Above all, a profoundly sincere man, as sincere as he is secret. He cannot bear the symbols that are found in his work, the theories that are elaborated out of his writings. When I say 'he cannot bear' I mean that he wants to ignore them, because I have never seen him in a rage. In any case, he refuses to be defined as a twentieth-century author, the head of an avant-garde. I think that he simply wants to be a man who knows how to observe and to understand. The universe that he describes is certainly his own, he lives it every day, and for him it is descriptive evidence itself.

One could work twenty hours a day with Beckett without ever seeing him relax or depart from his reserve. The best way to understand him is to read his works without looking for any philosophy other than a great human compassion. *Oh! Les Beaux Jours* is a marvellous love poem, the song of a woman who still wants to see and hear the man she loves. When I read the play for the first time I was overcome by it. I was reading everything that I had not dared to think since . . . since my first middle-aged wrinkle. And how quickly those wrinkles come!

It can seem cruel to play a Winnie, just as it can be cruel to cast any lucid glance on the human condition. It is true that no-one can go farther than *Oh! Les Beaux Jours*. At any rate, I do not think so.

I do not know what Beckett thinks of women, but I know that he understands them profoundly from the inside. If his plays manage to affect us and move us (and if they did not succeed in invading our sensibilities they would not be played throughout the entire world), it is because Beckett, in spite of his modesty, manages to express his immense compassion for all human life and because he is one of those exceptional men to whom love and lucidity are on the same level.

●

# My Dear Sam

ROBERT PINGET

---

My dear Sam,

John Calder has asked me to contribute to a book for your birthday. Well as I know that you do not particularly like this kind of tribute, I have accepted in order not to be missing from the circle of your closest friends.

One thing worries me and that is that Calder has suggested that I should write something on the 'mystique' of Beckett. It is a subject that seems to me impossible to tackle. And so to stay vaguely inside that framework I am dedicating to you this little text that you have known for a long time about a lady that we both love. Will that do?

Affectionately,

R

## SAINTE MARIE-MADELEINE

Poor Marie-Madeleine was very fond of the gentlemen. She was right of course, because we should love others, especially if they're able to help us out temporarily when times are hard. Because times were very hard, and you don't go in for that particular career if you're rolling in it. She was very fond of the gentlemen, but unfortunately they didn't return her love. You can't blame them too much, they were hardly in a position to saddle themselves with sentiments for a girl who was only good for you know what. And anyhow she needed something better. Bed's all very well for solving the problems of the immediate future, but from the knowledge you gain

84

there, something else is born, the desire in a good heart to increase that knowledge, to get to know everything, even to renounce the bed if it helps to penetrate into the other's heart a little better. It does not matter if you think of Marie-Madeleine on the Boulevard Sébastopol on an icy night huddled up in her rabbit-coat which she has already resewn fifteen times because it keeps on splitting under the arm, or around the Trastévère near a clip joint for Americans, smoking a cigarette, her skirt slit to the top of her thigh to attract the gaze of those whisky-sodden pigs, or else, in the district where the fez predominates, so colourful with its women in their beautiful dresses, their coal-like eyes and their half revealed breasts, drinking mint tea with a blind musician who has come to bring a little gaiety to the sadness of the flesh. In fact one can imagine her anywhere at all and anyhow at all. She has no personality of her own. But she did have the good luck to meet Jesus one evening when he was making a point of passing through her infamous district. As it is impossible to resist this man with his soft eyes, she went up to him and caught his attention. And he, he did not look at her with concupiscence. She suddenly felt embarrassed, something that had never happened to her before. They continued to look at each other. Then, all of a sudden, everything that Marie had lacked with her one-night stands, all her young girl's aspiration, all the goodness, the calm, the joy of loving, started to turn her head and she did not think any longer, but fell on her knees and cried like a madwoman, like the poor little mad girl that she was. One should not think that she was crying from shame, it would be better to think that she was crying from joy. She had found her man. He gives her his heart. It is all she needs. She has no further use for bodies, she has been more than saturated with them. And so she continued to cry from joy for many years, and never stopped pronouncing the name of her lover, and she is dead.

85

# *Beckett*

HAROLD PINTER

A short while ago, a friend of mine showed me a letter I had written to him in 1954. I had forgotten about it. It was about Beckett. Here is a paragraph from the letter:

'The farther he goes the more good it does me. I don't want philosophies, tracts, dogmas, creeds, way outs, truths, answers, *nothing from the bargain basement.* He is the most courageous, remorseless writer going and the more he grinds my nose in the shit the more I am grateful to him. He's not fucking me about, he's not leading me up any garden, he's not slipping me any wink, he's not flogging me a remedy or a path or a revelation or a basinful of breadcrumbs, he's not selling me anything I don't want to buy, he doesn't give a bollock whether I buy or not, *he hasn't got his hand over his heart.* Well, I'll buy his goods, hook, line and sinker, because he leaves no stone unturned and no maggot lonely. He brings forth a body of beauty. His work is beautiful.'

I can't, now, use any 'words' about his work at all, except to say that he seems to me far and away the finest writer writing.

# A Personal Note

CHARLES MONTEITH

---

No Irish writer has ever, I suspect, so notably failed to conform to the conventional picture of an Irish writer. Reserved and shy in manner; sparing in speech and correspondence; abstemious in habits; tall and impressively bony in appearance; courteous, punctilious and unfailingly prompt in dealing with business letters and with proofs—Beckett is among the least temperamental of authors. He is also among the most scrupulous, the most alert and most sensitive in his concern with meticulous textual accuracy, typography, the appearance of his work on the printed page; and yet he manages to convey this concern without being in the least finicky : and, when he is satisfied, is generous with praise.

During the ten years during which we* have published his plays—and his other short, dramatic pieces for stage, radio and television my liking and my respect for him have grown uninterruptedly. To publish his work is an honour of which any publishing house would be very proud. It is also, in the most genuine sense, a very great pleasure.

* Faber and Faber

# In Connection with Samuel Beckett

FERNANDO ARRABAL

In his work Beckett celebrates the ceremony of adventure and absence presided over by necessity and folly.

I think of Murphy, Malone, Molloy, for instance, and I feel the foundations, the exaggerations, the psalms, the faces bathed in tears, the old wandering pilgrim, the powerful master and the whole spectacle of our life hypnotised by the painter-philosopher.

Beckett, like Picasso, equals seven. Godot, like Kafka, equals five.

Whenever I read his plays, the book gives off a vapour of which the colours form the words 'HOW IT IS'.

If Beckett is speech, Godot will be rain. If Beckett lives in 'the signs of eternal evidence', Godot will live in 'the collective creation in honour of acrobatics'. And if Beckett becomes changed into Godot, Godot will have to play the principle role in the 'appearances of reality'.

In the everyday presence of the fantastic, Beckett, jumping out from behind the tombstones, brings to us the initiation, the hope and the despair. YES.

The writer has bequeathed to us the legend of legends.

We too, the writers of today, have learnt to write thanks to Beckett, as did Samuel Beckett himself.

The sensitive reality which he describes surrounds us and proclaims the necessity of the prodigious.

I am always fascinated by the magic mirror of this work, whose voice continues to call to me like giant days.

# A Propos Samuel Beckett

PHILIPPE STAIB

Winter 1964. Greek Street. THE ESTABLISHMENT. The first day's rehearsals. A month's work ahead and at the end of it *Endgame*.

The appointed time 9.00 o'clock. It's cold.

At 9.10 a taxi pulls up, a thin silhouette emerges and pays. My heart beats rapidly at the thought of the undertaking. Now at last to see this man at work.

A hasty greeting and we go in.

The actors, THESE ACTORS, embrace each other warmly. The play is difficult. It's cold.

Events seem to march by themselves. We start to read. The atmosphere from that instant is one of meditation and nothing else exists except the play.

Lunch time. There is already a journalist waiting. We have to talk to him.

He obviously wants to meet the author. He knows that he arrived in London the evening before. What to say to him?

On getting back the telephone is ringing and the demands for an interview multiply. No-one understands why every request to this young producer is unsuccessful, not how to measure the importance of this project of which I am at the same time proud and frightened.

Going outside where one has to prevent anyone entering the room where the rehearsal is taking place; on the one hand the probing, where is the great man? And on the other simplicity, research, work. Jackie asks 'Sam, how do I say to Hamm, "If I knew the combination of the safe, I'd kill you."?' He answers quietly, 'Just think that if you knew the combination of the safe, you would kill him.'

I have the very strong impression of looking at a train of events that all the participants have anticipated a long time ago, each one putting into the pool his own abilities with a mutual respect for the others. The value lies in the fact that each listens to the others with attention. The author and the actors are the heart of the enterprise, an indivisible heart. A wind of passion blows on them. The strength of the man is that he imposes his will without it ever being felt and without ever needing to insist. From the outside one can only have a profound desire to penetrate this closed universe, mingled with the certainty that such an ambition is impossible.

During all of this period, the other times that I've met him, I always get again the same impression of a calm simplicity, concentration, modesty, an indifference to anything that might affect him outside of his work. His work seems to come before everything and he seems to be the work. At the same time he has a profound sense of friendship, of respect for others, for those with whom he works, never a criticism, an attack, any aggressiveness.

It is difficult to say any more. Others have done so and better, but I should only like to bring to these pages the witness of a young man who can have nothing in common with Samuel Beckett and who has been fortunate enough to cross his path, keeping from those moments a profound respect for the authenticity of the man and his work, as well as of the manner in which the two blend together.

# Tribute

AIDAN HIGGINS

---

'*I have painted thought.*'—Poussin

The wind has died down in his work; no faces, no time of year, no time of day—only friction, for the time being at least. No rivers, no animals, no tides, no days, no faces, no faces; only movements, painful movements, sad accomplishments, common nouns manipulated by an overbearing intelligence. Some awkward implements, no periods, only mute (mute?) abstractions. No Celia, nor Moran, no Watt, no light, no cockel, no vetch, only mud, a mud of words ('sentinels of twilight . . . ghosts of this gloomy, fatal world'), coldness and reason.

Worlds once, now only words, uncharted places. Into this thin mist of words the most accomplished master of English prose since Joyce is disappearing. Very close to judgment, very close, too close. No edifying surroundings assuredly, no air to breathe. Fallen angels consort in the mud (*post hoc ergo propter hoc* Creation Day); a Genesis already hopelessly systematized, painful as geometry. Punishment before knowledge, persecution before history ('Man's fate, it seems, is to inscribe the figures of plane geometry on a spherical surface.' Professor Kenner *dixit*).

Sprat, prawn, rent sack, Pim, Bom (Boom?), fallen angels without memories to support them, baleful assuredly, a few sardines, a painful mimicry of sense, order, no breath of air, Pim, Boom, flounder on. Voices (presumably human?), victims, sing out of empty cisterns and exhausted wells. He has painted *poisson*.

91

*... from the next mortal to the next leading now here and saving corrections no other goal than the next mortal cleave to him give him a name train him up bloody him all over with Roman capitals gorge on his fables unite for life in stoic love to the last shrimp and a little longer ...*

(That civilization may not sink, its great battle lost ...)

That it is not aimless is evident. For his imperishable creations—Malone, Molloy, Moran, Krapp, Hamm, Clov, Vladimir, Estragon, Mr. and Mrs. Rooney, others—I salute him respectfully; this sixty-year-old unsmiling, not public man.

# *All the Livelong Way*

MARY HUTCHINSON

In May 1951 after an accident I happened to find myself in
New End Hospital, and seeing an announcement one day in
a paper I sent for a French book—it was *Molloy* by Samuel
Beckett. I had just heard of the author. I began to read and
went on with passion, for this book where moving thoughts
and drollery are combined in beautiful language, transformed
pain, trouble and Time. I still have the faint pencil copies
I made in bed of the passages I loved most.

In 1956 I sent to *The New Statesman* a comment on a criticism of *Molloy* in English, in which I said : 'the clue seems to
lie in the description of two men, A and C, going slowly towards each other; and in this vision of an approach, Moran
to Molloy, end to beginning, son to mother, A to C, (the out-
ward to the inward self) there is in truth "an indication of
what is to come", for the question Molloy asks : *What was I
doing there, and why come?* is vital in the whole work.'

The writer haunted by the fragmentation of all things, his
talisman veracity and sacrifice, has to dive deep into himself
in an attempt to find and to show himself, it seems to me, like
Shelley's *Prometheus Unbound* :

> 'To the deep, to the deep
> Down, down!
> Through the shades of sleep,
> Through the cloudy strife
> Of Death and of Life,
> Through the veil and the bar

93

Of things that seem and are
Even to the steps of the remotest throne
Down, down!

In *The Unnameable* the voice, or the writer, says *perhaps I am the tympanum, on the one side the outside, on the other the inside, that can be as thin as foil*. If so this instrument for recording experience is one of the most sensitive and truthful in existence.

Samuel Beckett sees Man with sympathy, simply as Didi and Gogo, or as the Shepherd turning towards his cottage, but sometimes as Mahu, Prince of Darkness.

He speaks of Time and Numbers, of Expression, of personal relationships, of Mortality and Immortality—

*the old questions!*

Put in a new way we could find perhaps new answers? But let us remember also in his work :

the melody of a past paradise (such as the landscapes, 'little scenes', love scenes, memories, the fadeless sea and flowers)—

the counterpoint of passion in the poems and of human pain (such as Mrs. Lambert's in *Malone Dies* and Bolton's in *Embers*) and baffled bravery (such as Winnie's in *Happy Days* and Molloy's as he perceives and perseveres in what he must do)—that are some of the variations in the main theme of this great symphony of Search, Revelation, Lament, and Hope *like a slate pencil* of blue in a sky of threatening cloud.

*J'y irais à l'issue, tôt ou tard, si je la disais là quelque part, les autres mots me viendraient, tôt ou tard, et de quoi pouvoir y aller, et y aller, et passer, à travers, et voir les belles choses que porte le ciel, et revoir les étoiles.*

It seems relevant to quote at this moment what Huysmans says in '*A Rebours*'.

'Of all forms of literature, the prose poem was Des Esseintes' favourite. Handled by an alchemist of genius it should, he

94

maintained, contain within its small compass and in concentrated form the substance of a novel . . .

Many were the times that Des Esseintes had pondered over the fascinating problem of writing a novel concentrated in a few sentences and yet comprising the cohobated juice of the hundreds of pages always taken up in describing the setting, drawing the characters, and piling up useful observations and incidental details . . .

In short, the prose poem represented in Des Esseintes' eyes the dry juice, the osmazome of literature, the essential oil of art.'*

Has not this foreseen form been attained today by Samuel Beckett in the alchemy of his tiny plays and last little books?

* Translation by Robert Baldick, Penguin Classics.

# Samuel Beckett

ALAN SIMPSON

It is said that genius is an infinite capacity for taking pains. If this is so, few Irish writers living or dead can really qualify for the title. Even Shaw's proliferations of ideas are frequently contradictory, Joyce's vivid imagery is often wrapped in mountains of obscure local verbiage and Wilde's adamantine wit is sometimes marred by purple patches of sticky Victoriana. However, from Sheridan to Behan their talents have flowed steadily eastwards across the Irish sea, flooding English letters with their rich, heady liquor. By birth, education and background Samuel Beckett is as Irish as the best of them, but he is different. In moving still further eastwards to the Continent early in his career, and by choosing to write in French, he imposed on himself the discipline of that symmetrical language. His translation of his own work as well as the prose and dialogue he has written directly in English, retain the astringency and polish which, according to Sartre, make him one of the leading stylists of Modern French.

In spite of their international fame, many Irish writers, like Wilde, only freed themselves from the parish pump of St. Patrick by transferring their allegiance to the parish pump of St. James. Beckett stands apart in this respect also. While a faint whiff of Anna Livia can always be detected in his writing by the expert and ardent Hibernophile, his abstract yet warmly human characters owe little to the manners of class or locality. His backgrounds are lunar in their austerity and strangeness. Beckett is truly non-parochial. He belongs to Europe and the world.

For precise dialogue, honed down to essentials, I commend him to all whose craft is the English language, particularly those who work in the dramatic media. It is because of this gift that I find his playwriting the most satisfying of all to direct.

At sixty, in Shavian terms at least, he has a long stint ahead of him. May he continue to explore the uncharted sources of his art and philosophy wherever they lead him. I know his mapping will be clear and firm. If we have the stamina we can follow him.

# *A Letter*

JOCELYN HERBERT

---

We asked Jocelyn Herbert to contribute and she has allowed us to print her letter.

Dear John,

Here is George's* contribution for your book of tributes for Samuel Beckett's 60th birthday. He is still unable to read or write himself, so he dictated it to me last night. As for myself, I do not feel really gifted enough with words to be able to write something which is not either pompous or patronizing, both of which would be more than usually unforgivable when writing about Sam. For me the wonderful thing about Sam is that the man is as remarkable and rare as his work, and both inevitably enrich and inspire all who have the good fortune to come in contact with them, in whatever capacity. Thank you for your kind enquiries about George. He has had the most awful time, and is still far from well. But we do hope the worst may be over at last, and that he will now get slowly stronger again, although it will be a very long time I'm afraid before he is anything like really well.

Best Wishes for 1966
Yours ever
Jocelyn

* George Devine.

# Last Tribute

GEORGE DEVINE

---

To meet Beckett for the first time must be described as the experience of a lifetime—it still is. But the first rule to be applied to the Beckett myth is avoidance of all vagueness and Cant. What do we really mean? We mean an experience, the like of which one has never experienced before, and which remains with one for ever in the memory. So it was with me. I spent half an hour with him in his flat in Paris. We talked, drank whiskey, and decided nothing. In that half hour I felt I was in touch with all the great streams of European thought and literature from Dante onwards. I just knew about all that by contact with this extraordinary mind and poetic vision; at the same time so rich and so simple. This man seemed to have lived and suffered so that I could see, and he was generous enough to pass it on to me. Generosity is the word that springs first to mind when thinking about this remarkable man.

# About the Contributors

JOHN CALDER  Managing Director of Calder & Boyars Ltd. who publish all of Samuel Beckett's work except the plays.

A. J. LEVENTHAL  Formerly Professor of English at Trinity College, Dublin, now living in Paris and assisting Samuel Beckett with business affairs.

MARIA JOLAS  American widow of Eugene Jolas, formerly editor of *Transition*, the influential English language literary review published from Paris in the '30's. She has been a leading translator and personality of the Parisian literary scene for many years.

JEROME LINDON  Head of Editions de Minuit, Samuel Beckett's French publisher.

MARCEL MIHALOVICI  Modern French composer of ballets and operas.

JACK MACGOWRAN  Northern Irish actor and specialist in Beckett roles.

HAROLD HOBSON  Drama critic of *The Sunday Times*.

JOHN FLETCHER  Lecturer in French and author of *The Novels of Samuel Beckett*. (Chatto & Windus 1965).

ALAN SCHNEIDER  American theatrical producer, specialising in plays by modern authors.

MARTIN ESSLIN  Literary critic and Head of Drama on B.B.C. Sound Radio. Author of *The Theatre of the Absurd* (Eyre and Spottiswoode)

HUGH KENNER  Professor of English at the University of Southern California and author of *Samuel Beckett* (Calder & Boyars 1962).

MADELEINE RENAUD  Distinguished French actress and co-director with Jean-Louis Barrault of the *Théâtre de France*.

ROBERT PINGET  French novelist and dramatist. Winner of the *Prix Femina* 1966.

HAROLD PINTER  Noted English actor and dramatist, author of *The Birthday Party*, *The Caretaker*, *The Homecoming*, etc.

CHARLES MONTEITH  Director of Faber & Faber who publish Samuel Beckett's plays.

FERNANDO ARRABAL  Younger French dramatist and novelist.

PHILIPPE STAIB  Theatrical producer responsible for the 1964 production of *Endgame* in Paris.

AIDAN HIGGINS  Younger Irish novelist. Author of *Langrishe, Go Down*, winner James Tait Black Memorial Prize, 1967.

MARY HUTCHINSON  English critic and editor of '*X*' *Magazine*.

ALAN SIMPSON  Irish theatrical producer.

JOCELYN HERBERT  Stage designer.

GEORGE DEVINE  English actor and producer and late director of The English Stage Company.

AVIGDOR ARIKHA  Israeli painter.

HENRI HAYDEN  French landscape painter.